M000306253

# Live Outside the Box

## Laura Riviezzo-Taggart

TRILOGY CHRISTIAN PUBLISHERS

*TUSTIN, CA*

Trilogy Christian Publishers

A Wholly Owned Subsidiary of Trinity Broadcasting Network

2442 Michelle Drive

Tustin, CA 92780

For information, address Trilogy Christian Publishing

Rights Department, 2442 Michelle Drive, Tustin, Ca 92780.

Trilogy Christian Publishing/ TBN and colophon are trademarks of Trinity Broadcasting Network.

For information about special discounts for bulk purchases, please contact Trilogy Christian Publishing.

Manufactured in the United States of America

10 9 8 7 6 5 4 3 2 1

Library of Congress Cataloging-in-Publication Data is available.

ISBN 978-1-64773-498-5

ISBN 978-1-64773-499-2 (ebook)

# Contents

# Dedication

I dedicate this book to my two sons, Ronnie and Jonathan.

They have been my rock throughout my endeavors. Without their support and assistance, this book could not have come to fruition.

I love them both so much more than any words could express.

# Acknowledgements

I want to thank all my patients whose names have been deleted or changed for anonymity. Only those who've given me permission to use their names did I use. I want to thank all my family and friends, and acquaintances for whom, without you, this book would not have been possible. A special thanks to my son Ronnie, the computer whiz who helped me get this book on Microsoft word and placed on a USB flash drive. A special thanks to my son, Jonathan, for giving me Amazon dot, so I could listen to "The Message" as I wrote, and thanks to both of them for their photographs and support.

Special thanks to my friends, Renuka, Loretta, Raeann, Rose, Judy, Richard, Amber, Tee, and my sister Christine for their stories and encouragement throughout this endeavor. I also want to thank everyone at both my bible groups of past and present for providing me the opportunity to study the Word. I want to thank everyone at TBN and EWTN for their inspiration and confirmation during the writing of this book. And I want to express gratitude to the Holy Spirit for giving me the wisdom, knowledge, and courage to write His book.

I want to thank the Shrine of Our Lady of the Island in Manorville, New York, for the peace I've always found there and for the pictures I've taken from there.

# Preface

The American Psychiatric Nurses Association (APNA), of whom I am a member, made a statement that implied that the psychiatric mental health nurse must think outside the box in caring for our mentally ill. And I thought that while this is true... *Why can't we all "Live outside the box"* (outside the norms of this world) because, with God, all things are possible.

All things are possible for one who believes.

(Mark 9:23 ESV)

**Dare** to live outside the conformity
of this world...
Dream a dream... with the grace of God
It will be fulfilled, according to His plan...
Surrender your life to God and...
Watch what He can do with it;
You will be surprised.
DARE to...
*Live Outside the Box.*

LAURA RIVIEZZO-TAGGART

# Introduction

This book has been written for you—All of you. This book has been written not only for believers but for nonbelievers as well.

This book was not written to offend any one religion, nor any attempt to sway one from their faith into another. This book was written for Christians, Catholics, Born-agains, Baptists, Lutherans, Pentecostals, Jews, Hindus, Muslims, Buddhists, Agnostics, and Atheists.

I believe in evangelization, and this is my testament. We all have a story to tell if we just listen. We all need to spread the "Good News," the gospel to the ends of the earth. This has always been our command. This book has been my way.

While some parts you may believe and others not so much, all incidents are true and are accounts of the people and places as I've encountered them along my journey called... Life. So, take what you will and believe what you may. May God bless you.

I believe that this book has been the Holy Spirit inspired and directed. He confirmed His book at every turn with confirmations. I'd just finish a chapter when no sooner a priest or pastor would come on TV, saying what I had just written. Sometimes in Bible group, the same passage would be reiterated that I just wrote. Without Him, it would not have been written. It was written by Him for You.

I am nothing; I am but an instrument, a tiny pencil in the hands of the Lord with which He writes what He likes. However imperfect we are, He writes beautifully.

—Mother Teresa[1]

It is a testimony of God, alive and well in this world.

Just as the light always overcomes the darkness, good always triumphs over Evil.

---

1 "Mother Teresa Quote." n.d. Quotefancy. Accessed August 4, 2020. https://quotefancy.com/quote/868994/Mother-Teresa-I-am-nothing-I-am-but-an-instrument-a-tiny-pencil-in-the-hands-of-the-Lord.

CHAPTER 1

# Beautifully Broken

*Lord, I come to you broken and shattered*
*like glass on the ground in so many pieces, but then...*
*The Sunlight shines through each broken piece illuminat-*
*ing radiant light and sparkle into so many different colors*
*and directions, all emanating from the same broken glass.*
*Thank you, Jesus, for showing us light in our brokenness,*
*equating it to hope. Like the lighthouse, a Beacon of Hope*
*shining the light amidst the darkness,*
Hope Anchors the Soul.

(Hebrews 6:19)

If you look closely at an anchor, it resembles a "J" for
Jesus, (our hope) on the cross, the anchor to our Soul.

*Beautifully Broken* is also the name of a lovely song
sung by Plumb.[2] It describes it perfectly. And let's face
it, we're all somewhat "broken". Nobody has it all to-

---

2 "Beautifully Broken by Tiffany Arbuckle Lee, and Jenny Slate Lee,
2018." n.d. *Wikipedia, The Free Encyclopedia.* https://en.wikipedia.
org/wiki/Plumb_(singer).

gether. By "brokenness," I mean something tangible or intangible that has happened to you and has shaken you to your very core. Something that feels awry on the inside, deep down in the inner depths of our heart and soul, even though you could look totally together on the outside. It could be a divorce, an abandonment, an emotional or physical loss of some kind, a victim of violence or abuse, an addiction, some sort of trauma, or depression. Whatever you have been through or are going through, there is no such place that God cannot reach in and pull you out of.

Do not think that you or I are too insignificant or broken to be used by God to do His work on this earth. We are all God's children! And the good news is that we are loved by an awesome God. We may not all be saints, but we are all sinners. We must know that God loves us anyway. He sent His son Jesus Christ to die for our sins, and He did so willingly. He spared Abraham from sacrificing his only son Isaac and rewarded him with descendants as many as the stars in the sky (Genesis 20:11, 17). St. Paul (Saul, as he was then called) sought out Christians to kill them. He literally "Saw the Light" when he was knocked off his horse and blinded! (Acts 9:3–8). God got his attention! He then went on to write approximately two-thirds of the New Testament. St. Peter, who denied Jesus not once, but three times was forgiven, and he was given the Keys to the Kingdom

(Luke 22:61; Matthew16:19). Even the Son of God, Jesus Christ, was betrayed by one of His friends, Judas, to die (Luke 22:48). The loneliness in which He must have felt! Because at the foot of the cross, standing there was only His favorite friend, John, His mother, and two others (John 19:25). He chose to die anyway, for us, for our sinfulness and brokenness.

Have you ever felt like you don't measure up or that you're just not good enough? Have you ever felt bad because someone did something mean to you or just left you out? Most of us have felt down and out about something, sometime in our lives. Listening to Pastor Charles Stanley's sermon, I interpreted that, Brokenness is where God finds us and chooses us for His maximum usefulness.[3]

God chooses the unqualified, the sinners, the lost, the forgotten to lead the so-called "qualified people". God usually uses the average "Joe" to do his work, not famous athletes, movie actors or actresses, kings, or queens. Just regular people, like you and me. There are many examples of this in the Bible: Moses had a speech impediment and was a murderer, but God used him anyway to ask Pharaoh to let his people go. Moses did lead his people, the Israelites, out of Egypt.[4] David, a mere shepherd boy, killed a giant named Goliath, with

---

3 Exodus 2:12, 4:10, 5:1, 12:41.
4 1 Samuel 1, 17:15, 17:50; 2 Samuel 2:4, 11:3–4.

just his faith and a slingshot. Later he went on to be king. But even King David was not perfect. He not only had an affair with a married woman but also had her husband killed.[5] Then there was Joseph, who was sold into slavery by his own brothers. Talk about broken. Then he was imprisoned for something he did not even do before he became second in charge only to Pharaoh. While he was in power, instead of punishing his brothers, he forgave them.[6] Then there was Jonah, who was told by God to go to Nineveh, a place he didn't want to go to or was afraid to go to, but went in the opposite direction! (Jonah 1:2). Could you imagine God telling you to do something and you refuse? It's no wonder he found himself in the belly of a giant fish for three days! (Jonah 2:1).

Everyone has a story to tell. No matter how great or humble, you can find goodness in everyone. You just have to look hard and long enough to see it.

Everyone has a story of their own... If we only take the time to listen...

I, myself, am a beautifully broken, divorced, single mother of two. I was not "saintly" before my marriage at age thirty-one years of age. Let's be honest. I wasn't living the godly life back then either. In the '70s and '80s, it was still the "Love the one you're with" mentality

---

5  Genesis 38:28, 39:20, 41:40, 45:15.
6  Stanley, 2014.

of the world. It was sinful. Also, living with your spouse before marriage was called "living in sin". I was very broken when in 2005, my husband left me for another woman.

I remember that night like it was yesterday. He did not want to make love. I asked, "What's wrong?"

He replied, "I don't love you anymore."

I said, "What? You just don't wake up one day and say, I don't love you anymore." I then instinctively asked, "Who is she?"

He said, "Someone I met at one of my truck stops."

I asked him if he slept with her, and he said with a smile on his face, "Well, we've done stuff in my truck" (the new Chevy Silverado.)

I wanted to get this straight. So... making love to me would be cheating on her? I said, "You need to leave."

He left that night but returned for a couple of weeks and slept on the couch until he could find a place. The devastation, the loss, the sense of betrayal, and the grief were overwhelming. He left two days before Valentine's Day, and I was hurt beyond all imagination. I told my sons that "Daddy had a heart attack (which he did), and sometimes people need some time to process it and their life's priorities." I could not bring it to myself to tell them the truth. Later, my twelve-year-old said, "I heard him talking on the phone saying, I love you to someone, and I knew it wasn't you."

In shock and disbelief, I just looked at my son. What words could I say? He knew the truth. Kids always do. He also knew the hurting I was going through. Even at just twelve years old... he came and kept me company some nights because neither he nor I wanted to believe what happened or to feel alone.

I worked as many hours as I could to make ends meet. My ex was not forthcoming with the child support payments. It was a very tough time, both financially and emotionally. I endured a deep depression as I worked many overtime shifts to provide for the needs of my children, including paying the mortgage payments and keeping them in Catholic high school. Three years later, I met a man, a drummer in a band where "sex, drugs, and rock-n-roll" came into play. Again, holding on to a shred of faith, living the "unclean sinful life," it took a catastrophe to happen to awaken me from that way of life.

It was November 1, 2008. My oldest son was away in another state in college when at three a.m., I received his phone call. Apparently, he had gotten into some trouble with some kids at school. I immediately got on the nine a.m. ferry to get to him. I prayed and cried the whole way.

Fast forward, heading home hysterically crying, I called one of my best friends, Judy, who said she knew of a good lawyer in that state, the best. I called him, and he took the case for $2,500, of which I had to borrow $2,000 from my youngest brother. For two years, we had numerous court dates with hotel and ferry expenditures and court cancellations. I prayed every night to God and the blessed virgin to spare my son from this nightmare. I asked our Blessed Mother, "I know you loved your son, Jesus Christ, as much if not more than I love my nineteen-year-old son. Please pray to keep him safe in this situation." She heard my prayers, and although it was a rough two years of not knowing, just praying and hoping and believing for the best! The lawyers' office waited for five years until I could pay him the last $2,500 I owed them, without once sending me a bill! My prayers were answered above and beyond what I could have ever imagined or asked for.

In the midst of all this turmoil, God knew I needed a "time out," I'll call it. I went on a leave of absence from my job. My sister Christine came to stay with us for a time. Between the stress and demands of running a Psychiatric Emergency Room, going through menopause, my son's problem at college, a break-up with the boyfriend, financial difficulties, balancing work, and home life, I was physically, mentally, emotionally, and spiritually exhausted.

I needed some time away from the demands and stresses of all of it. I now knew that with Him and the prayers of many, that is what would see me through.

I returned to church and began reading and meditating on His Word. It was a wake-up call that slapped me in the face telling me, "Time for A Change" from God Himself. It took the love of my family and a handful of praying friends and the Lord to get me back on my feet again. I returned to work five months later, after much prayer, visits to the Shrine of Our Lady, confessions, repentance, mercy, and grace. God is always faithful.

With much trepidation, I returned to work as a supervisor of the Psychiatric Emergency Room of a large hospital. As with anywhere you work, there were the ones who couldn't wait to see me fail, and those who were my prayer warriors. I said the Serenity Prayer every morning:

*Lord, grant me the serenity to accept the things I cannot change, the courage to change the things I can and the wisdom to know the difference.*[7]

I would have a conversation with God every morning on my way to work in the forty-five-minute car ride asking for wisdom and to be able to provide the best care to both my patients and staff. This time, I knew I had "Him" as my backup. This gave me hope and strength

7 "Serenity Prayer by Reinhold Niebuhr, 1951." 2020. *Wikipedia, The Free Encyclopedia.* 2020. https://en.wikipedia.org/wiki/Serenity_Prayer.

to get through each day as with the support of my nurse manager and the director of nurses. All things are possible with God! (Matthew 19:26).

So, God put the pieces of the glass back together... one at a time, one day at a time. I am one of the beautifully broken people God continued to use for His glory. I retired one and a half years later. Eight months after I retired from the hospital, I obtained a job as a psychiatric nurse for a home healthcare agency. I continued to bring faith and hope to those who felt "broken" into their own homes and love them just as Jesus would have.

Who knew better than me what real depression is? I knew all too well what it felt like, looked like, and acted like. Who better than I could relate, empathize, and understand, having gone through it myself? I now knew what the words, "And we know that all things work together for good to those who love God, to those who are called according to His purpose," really means (Romans 8:28 NKJV). This was now my mission—To share my wisdom, faith, life experiences, both good and bad, to help others get through... to see hope... to see the light at the end of the tunnel.

Saint Faustina was told by the Lord, "Tell aching mankind to snuggle close to my Merciful heart, and I will fill it with peace."[8]

*The Lord is close to the brokenhearted...*

(Psalm 34:18 NIV)

*He heals the brokenhearted and binds up their wounds.*

(Psalm 147:3 ESV)

The song *God Only Knows* by For King and Country is a powerful song. As a home health care psychiatric nurse, I recall several of my patients whom I'd call broken.

There was Jay. She had two children. She had a neurological disorder and a mood disorder. She fought very hard for herself and her family. She would be on the phone with her doctors' offices and insurance companies, trying to get appointments in order. I saw her bathroom shower curtain one day and noticed it had "Praise the Lord, Trust in the Lord," written on it. I asked her about her faith, and she told me she was a born-again Christian and still had her trust in God to get her through. She even finished an online Christian

---

8 Kosicki, Rev. George W. 2003. Divine Mercy Answers Life's Crises and Problems. C.S.B. quotes from the Diary of St. Faustina used with permission of the Marians of the Immaculate Conception, Eden Hill, Stockbridge, MA. https://www.renewalministries.net/files/freeliterature/DM Answers life crises and problems.pdf.

minister course. With a change in her medications, she would sometimes have an unsteady gait and blurred vision. I reminded her, "For we walk by faith, not by sight," and we laughed (2 Corinthians 5:7 ESV). I admired her strength. At times because her memory was affected, she had forgotten an appointment. I listened to her struggles and assisted her by making some phone calls, checking her neurological status, and her blood pressure. One day she, very matter-of-factly, told me that she didn't have much money this year to buy her kids Christmas presents, not that she was looking for a handout, she just said that "They will just have to understand." I left her home that day feeling sad. That night the Holy Spirit gave me the idea to go shopping for her two kids at the $5.00 and under store. I bought several items and wrapped them, and gave them to her to give to her kids for Christmas. After many visits and many talks of God, she finally obtained an aide to help her with activities of daily living for a couple of hours a day. We are chosen by God to be right where we are, when we are, to bring some hope and joy to another.

"Be someone's miracle," as Joel Osteen would imply.[9] "God blesses us to be a blessing to others," as Pas-

---

9 "Joel Osteen – Become a Miracle." 2014. Sermonly. 2014. http://www.sermonly.com/14/joel-osteen-become-a-miracle/7014/.

tor Robert Morris would say.[10] I think they are right. It's just another way of saying "Love One Another," as Jesus would say (John 13:34 ESV).

I met a man in his early thirties, married with his wife and two young children. He was a chef and owner of a prominent pizzeria. He had a glioblastoma, an inoperable aggressive malignant brain tumor, and he needed to talk to someone—Someone not of his family. We spoke about treatment and side effects and that he had paid off his mortgage with his business. He was glad that he had made plans for them financially, but he was not yet ready to die.

I then asked him, "Do you have any faith?"

He said, "Yes, I'm Catholic."

I said to him, "Well, you know it's not over until He says it's over! God works miracles all the time. Pray for one. It can't hurt," and we chuckled.

I asked him to believe and trust and have faith, go to confession, or whatever he needs to do to be at peace with his God. And I told him, "You need to make the most of every single moment you have with your wife and kids."

---

10 "Living Beyond Blessed by Pastor Robert Morris: Gateway Church." 2019. Gateway Church. 2019. https://gatewaypeople.com/series/beyond-blessed.

The following week I saw him again, and he was in a better frame of mind. We spoke about being Italian and how important food was to us.

He said, "Do you think I should invite my family over for Sunday dinner, and I'll cook meatballs with macaroni and gravy for them?"

I said, "Absolutely!" I teased, "Are you any good?"

He said, "Absolutely! Come to my restaurant and order anything you want. It's on me." I left there knowing the Holy Spirit had intervened, giving me the right words at the right time, offering hope to this man and a peace that surpasses all understanding (Philippians 4:7). I never did get my free meal, but I'm sure he was a good chef. I got in my car and cried.

I remember the first year that I had to work Christmas Eve so I could have Christmas Day off. For years I'd refuse to work Christmas eve or day because this was my holiday to enjoy, and working it, I found it was very depressing.

I was sent to this family home where the mom had dementia, and the dad had liver cancer, a man in his eighties. His daughter was caring for both of them, and being the sole caregiver was very stressful. There wasn't much I could do for her father, who spoke only Italian, so the daughter interpreted for me to find out if he had any pain. He said, "No." His daughter had his medications under control. I could sense the daughter wanted to talk, so in the hallway on my way out, I asked her if she was alright. This opened up a floodgate of tears. She needed to talk about her feelings. She didn't want her Dad to have to suffer any more treatments at this stage, just make him comfortable with his family at his side. I applauded her for her strength and courage. I saw the statue of the Blessed Virgin as I entered and asked about her faith. She said, "Yes, I pray the Rosary all the time." I recommended her to "Go to the Shrine of Our Lady, you will find peace and consolation there, and Father R. is a great person to talk to." I told her I would pray for both her and her family. She thanked me, and by this time, we were both in tears. That is why I do not like to work on Christmas Eve or day.

Another patient of mine was a twenty-year-old man who also had a history of addiction. I was there because he had mentioned suicide to another nurse. I sat with him, and we talked. I instructed him about his Insulin usage. I asked him how he was managing and if he was going to any meetings (Alcoholics anonymous or narcotics anonymous). I asked him about his plans. He talked a little at first, but after three hours of talking, he admitted to me that he, in fact, did take too much insulin.

I said to him, "It appears to me that you are sad and that maybe you took that much insulin in an effort to kill yourself."

He said, "You are right."

I immediately called his doctor, who decided he needed to go to the emergency room. His family member took him. I thank God that He gave me the right words and intuition to make the right call.

I wrote on November 2014 in my journal:

*The Lord, my God, give me*
*The strength, courage, and grace*
*To minister to those in pain,*
*Suffering and despair....*
*Sharing His light in the darkness,*
*Serving those in my care...*
*With compassion and Love,*
*Bringing only Hope and Peace.*
*Amen.*

After I returned from Ireland with my eldest son, Ronnie, I met an Irish man in his eighties, who had never married, no children, and lived alone in his trailer. He was in a well-maintained trailer park on the Eastern end of Long Island. He had a few neighbors who checked in on him from time to time. I was sent to see him because of a recent depression episode, which resulted in a short hospitalization. It appeared that a neighbor came to check in on him and found he hadn't moved from his bed in days. He did not eat or drink anything, and they called 911.

We started talking, and he was a Catholic and did not believe in suicide. But... if it happened by dehydration or natural causes because he hadn't taken any of his heart medications either... could he then not be held responsible? I sat and talked to him many times about passive suicide that was brought about by his depression. He owned a car, but it was winter and unsafe to drive due to snow and ice. So, due to hazardous conditions, he was mostly homebound. His neighbors checked in on him and brought over some food.

It turns out he never did learn how to cook except heating up can food or microwaveable foods. Teaching was done pertaining to canned foods and frozen foods that have a high sodium count, which is not good for his high blood pressure. We spoke about his faith, he also said he believed, and he was old school Catholic. He prayed his rosary every night, and he showed them to me. I told him, "God loves you very much, and He is NOT ready for you to go home yet." Remember, "God helps those who help themselves. "Go food shopping in your car when the weather permits and look for low salt food or cold cuts. "

A few weeks later, full of pride, he showed me that he bought low sodium soups (Hey, it's a start). I gave him a cross, which I brought from St. Patricks' Cathedral in Ireland on the last day of my visit. I said, "Keep the Faith." He thanked me and said he would miss me. I miss him. It's days like this that I knew God sent me to where I could make a difference.

One year, for Nurses Day at the hospital, I made cards for all the staff, nurses, nurses' aides, and nursing station clerks with my motto. There was a picture of a big pink heart on the front, and it read:

*NURSING...*

*Making a Difference...*

*One Day at a Time...*

*One Life at a Time...*

The inside stated, "*Thank you for making a difference.*"

I was inspired by the Star Thrower story:

One day a man was walking along the beach when he noticed a boy hurriedly picking something up and gently throwing things into the ocean.

Approaching the boy, he asked, "Young man, what are you doing?"

The boy replied, "Throwing starfish back into the ocean. The surf is up, and the tide is going out. If I don't throw them back, they'll die."

The man laughed to himself and said, "Don't you realize that there are miles and miles of beach and hundreds of starfish? You can't make a difference!"

> After listening politely, the boy bent down, picked up another starfish, and threw it into the surf. Then, smiling at the man, he said, "I made a difference to that one."[11]

I love this story because, yes, you can make a difference even if you are only one person! And that one person will be better off because of it. As Mother Theresa said, "We can only do small things with great love."[12] You can be the light in the darkness! There's a saying that asks, "God, why don't you do Something?" His answer was, "I did; I made You." Be that change. You alone can make a difference.

Like everyone else, there are days I'd like to quit. I think I can't do this anymore. I have nothing more to give. Then a song will come on "The Message" from SiriusXM radio, and it pushes me to keep going. Every song is usually right on time for me. I've said to God, "I'm not a quitter. You got me this job. You'll tell me when it's time to quit." I was making good money (blood money). I was paying off all my bills, driving a new car, bought my sons' new cars, and went on vacations with my boys

---

11 "The Star Thrower by Loren Eisely, 1969." 2019. *Wikipedia, The Free Encyclopedia*. 2019. https://en.wikipedia.org/wiki/The_Star_Thrower.
12 "Quote by Mother Teresa." 2016. Catholic News Service. 2016. https://www.catholicnews.com/services/englishnews/2016/mother-teresa-do-small-things-with-great-love.cfm.

overseas. If you had asked me five years ago if any of this could have been possible, I would not have believed any of it. I also would not have believed that I could minister to people in their homes. But because God is good, all the time. He, once again, gave me more than I could have ever asked for or believed for.

I met a seventy-year-old Vietnam veteran who had kidney cancer for twenty years. Now it had metastasized to his bones. We talked about faith and how God had given him these twenty years to live. Now he was dying. When I asked him how he felt about it, he replied, "It's OK. I have too many people waiting for me up in heaven."

I said to him, "Wow, what great faith and trust you have."

As I was leaving, he said to me, "Shine on Lady."

A tear fell from my eye that day as it was confirmation that I was shining Jesus' light into the world.

In 2015, I wrote my thoughts:

*Life... It's Not the Destination. It's the Journey.*

*Life is a lot like driving...*

*You think you know where you are going*

*And when you will get there*

*And hope you get to where you have to go...*

*But... sometimes we get a flat tire,*

*Which prolongs us from getting there...*

*And sometimes, we hit unexpected detours or speed bumps, which we did not anticipate.*

*And sometimes we have to make a U-turn, or even stop, Because we've gotten lost along the Way.*

*Even when we know the Way.*

*Some days it is foggy, and the Way isn't so clear...*

*And sometimes, it's difficult to see the road ahead...*

*But if we just say a prayer and let "Jesus take the wheel."*[13]

*We can just put our trust in*

*Him to SHOW us the WAY.*

---

13 "Carrie Underwood 'Jesus Take the Wheel,' 2005." 2020. *Wikipedia, The Free Encyclopedia.* 2020. https://www.musicnotes.com/sheetmusic/mtd.asp?ppn=MN0053248.

CHAPTER 2

# Answered Prayers

God answers prayers. As a matter of fact, He's been doing it for years now. And He's not going to stop now. He answered Daniel's prayer in the lion's den and shut the mouths of lions (Daniel 6:22). He saved Shadrach, Meshach, and Abednego from the seven times hotter furnace (Daniel 3:19), which King Nebuchadnezzar threw them into because they refused to worship his god (Daniel 3:25). But, the King said, "Look! I see four men loosed and walking about in the midst of the fire without harm, and the appearance of the fourth is like a son of the gods!" (Daniel 3:92 NASB). They sang and blessed God and prayed. Moses prayed, and God sent him manna from heaven—quail, and water from a rock (Exodus 16:4, 13; 17:6). Prayer matters. Prayer makes a difference. His answer may be "Yes." It may be "Not now," or it may be "I've got better things in store for you," as I've heard one pastor say.

In my personal life, prayer has made a difference since I was a little girl, and I even prayed for a bicycle. I was in third grade, and I did not know how to ride a bicycle. A nun gave me the coloring book of St. Bernadette of Our Lady of Lourdes and how Our Lady appeared to her. I prayed to Our Lady on my walk to school. I prayed for a bicycle. Sound silly? It was, but it happened! That Christmas, I got an army green bicycle (my father had spray painted it) with a white basket in front. I was overjoyed and knew from then that prayers are answered. Since then, I've had numerous occasions of prayers being answered.

When I was seventeen years old, our family had moved to North Carolina into the projects. I constantly prayed to move back to N.Y. to where my friends and family were. About three months later, my father said, "I think we will move back to N.Y."

I said out loud, "Thank you, God!"

My father said, "What do you mean?"

So, I told him, "I've been praying so very much to return to N.Y."

He said, "Well, I guess it was you He was listening to and not me." That's when I really got it, at age seventeen, that God hears prayers and answers them. We moved back to N.Y.

One time my brother's daughter was in Neonatal Intensive care because of a common problem during childbirth. One night, when I was working at the same hospital, I was allowed to see her. I prayed over her and said, "Mommy and Daddy love you soooo very much. And God loves you too. So, you get well soon." She is a beautiful, young, married lady today.

When my sister got cervical cancer before she was thirty years old, I prayed that she would be ok. She had surgery and did not require any chemotherapy or radiation treatments! Her church members came and laid hands on her as well. It was a group effort. "For where two or three have gathered together in My name, I am there in their midst," said Jesus (Matthew 18:20 NASB). She has been cancer-free for thirty years now.

I remember shopping in a flea market with Judy, one of the nurses I worked with, for Christmas presents. It was in the city. When we arrived at her house, her phone rang (this was before we had cell phones). I was told, "There's been a terrible accident, your son, Ronnie, has been airlifted to the hospital. I know nothing about the extent of his injuries. Both your husband and your other son were sent to another hospital." I whispered and cried out to God, "Please let him be ok. He's only ten years old!"

I drove frantically to the hospital, praying the whole time. The EMT's said that "No one should have survived that crash." The EMT's cut my son out of the back of my husband's pickup that was molded around a telephone pole. His head was bleeding, and they airlifted him to the hospital. I arrived at the hospital in such a state until I saw my son sitting up on a stretcher with staples in his head, talking! Praise God! The ER doctor told me that they CT Scanned his entire body, and there were no injuries anywhere, no broken bones either! I was so relieved. "Thank you, God!" I took my son home that night and was so grateful.

Days later, I asked my sons individually about that day. Each recounted the fact that (while their father was unconscious) an old lady came to them and told them that everything would be ok and then vanished. I believe they were visited by an angel.

Growing up in a traditional Catholic home, I was baptized, made Holy Communion, and confirmation.

We went to church every Sunday (mass was in Latin), so very little was understood. I remember going to Catechism classes with the nuns and memorizing prayers. I also remember the nuns lending me a white dress for communion. I thought that at every mass, a miracle was performed and that God knew just how many hosts to make for each person receiving communion that day.

I was one of the very few who adored the nuns. They gave me my first guitar lessons. I remember my father getting me an old Spanish guitar with the F-holes on each side at a garage sale! I loved music, and later it was my escape. I would learn new songs all the time. Fortunately, in 1972, my sister and I joined a folk group at mass and played and sang. We were before our time playing songs like *The Sounds of Silence* and *Let It Be*. We even went and made an album! It was one of the best times of my life. So, God was in my life at a very young age.

My good friend Rose's brother, Richard, came from Haiti to live with her in 2008. In 2010, a devastating earthquake hit Haiti. Richard was about eleven years old. He had a half-sister living with his mother. His mother was killed, leaving Kim an orphan in Haiti. Kim was about seven years old.

With the help of another friend who had adopted children from other countries, my friend Rose and I were able to get Kim to a caretaker's home for a specified amount of money each month. Then adoption became impossible due to the fact there were too many kidnappings of children and then crossing them over the border to the Dominican Republic for slave trafficking. The U.S. government deemed it unsafe to go to Haiti because of its unstable government, and it appeared to be a hopeless situation. Then I started to have a bad feeling about Kim's safety with these caretakers, and my friend Rose said she did too. We started to pray for an answer.

We started to look up orphanages in Haiti on the internet. I looked into Catholic Relief Center, Habitat for Humanity, and various other orphanages and schools. A few weeks later, Rose was working a 1 to 1 for a patient (that means one staff to one patient ratio), and the curtain was drawn closed to the person next to her patient. A nurse came in and asked if she spoke French, and could she interpret for the lady next to her? Rose was glad to help. It turns out that the woman was from Haiti with a blood clot in her leg. She just so happened to be the Mother Superior of the orphanage in Haiti and had agreed to take Kim under her wing for the cost of her uniform and books only. It was like a miracle! God put that nun and my friend in the same room for a reason. There are no co-incidents, just God incidents.

Fast forward to 2012, on vacation to Panama with my two sons aged twenty and twenty-three years of age. It was a hot, beautiful day, the sun was shining, and we decided to go ATV-ing (all-terrain vehicle), when I spotted a statue of Our Lady set quite a distance off the road in the thick brush. I quickly said a little prayer.

We each got a four-wheeled ATV. My eldest son, Ron, and I had ridden on one of these before, but my youngest son, Jonathan, had not. The terrain going up the mountainside was both beautiful, as it was treacherous. On one side of this dirt and rocky road was the edge of the mountain with no guard rails or fence, just a huge drop as far as the eye could see of trees and rocks. We climbed higher and higher with our guide, Christian, in front. I was at the end, watching out for everyone's safety. Apparently, the two women we were with had never driven on one before either. When we finally arrived at the beautiful waterfall, we were eager to jump in with our now sweaty bodies. It was so worth it. It was so refreshing!

Now on the way down was another story. I was now in front and my eldest son Ron at the back, then one woman, then Jonathan, and the other woman. The dangerous side was now on the right of us. I was confident my eldest son, Ron, could handle anything since everyone did ok on the way up. Surely the way down would be easier? All of a sudden, I see the women behind me get off and start running down the hill, screaming. I was at an incline and did not have enough room to turn the ATV around. I knew instantly that there was something terribly wrong with one of my sons! I whispered to Our Lady, "Please, Mother of God, don't let one of my sons fall off the cliff. Please watch over him like you did your Son. You know I love them as much as you did Jesus. Please, I beg you to keep them safe."

I started screaming for Christian, the guide who did not speak any English, over and over again. Finally, he shows up, and I point down the hill. I finally turned the quad off and began running down the hill also, afraid of what I might find. As I got there, I found my youngest son, Jonathan, in a ravine off the side of the mountain with Christian and Ronnie lifting the quad off of his leg as he was pinned down by the weight of it. He told me later he attempted to let one of the women to go ahead of him and had moved over slightly when the wheels of the ATV slipped on rocks into the ravine, tipping it over onto him. I thank God there was a ravine at that precise spot and not the edge of the cliff. Thank you, Blessed Mother and Jesus, for saving my son that day!

Years later, I met a man, well into his eighties, and his wife. I don't remember his physical ailment, but his story is even more miraculous. He told me that his mother always prayed to Our Lady Mary. She prayed that he would not have to go off to war, but he was drafted and had to go, anyway. One week before he was to leave, his brother said, "Let's play a game of basketball." He told me, "I really didn't want to play ball. I wanted to see my girlfriend (who happens to be his wife), but I played anyway. Don't you know, I broke my wrist and had to go to an army hospital and therefore wasn't qualified to go off to war! My mother's prayers were answered."

He then told me one night he saw the Blessed Virgin. He described her as a bright shining light with the most beautiful voice you could ever imagine, and she told him that whatever he asked of her, she would grant. He asked to "Stick around a couple of more years." Afraid I would think he was crazy, I did not for one-second doubt this man's vision. It was the way he told me of it, so peaceful, yet so full of hope and confidence. Since I was a little girl, I wondered what it would be like to have Our Lady appear to me.

I had a patient who reported to me that she was sexually abused while in the hospital by two aides while she was coming out of anesthesia. Although she could not remember the details, she did make a police report and told her husband about it. Now she came home, and it consumed her. She could not eat, sleep, or carry out her daily functions; she was afraid to go outside or open her front door. It appeared she might be suffering from post-traumatic stress disorder, commonly known as PTSD. I was called to talk to her. I told her that "This was a horrific ordeal that no one should have to go through. I'm sorry this happened to you." I told her there are several pastors on TV that speak about letting go and letting God handle it. I told her that sometimes God blocks our memory when it is too painful to remember, to protect us. It remains in our subconscious. I explained to her about PTSD and hinted at a therapist who specializes in this sort of thing.

The next time I saw her, she was doing better. She said she had seen one of the pastors on TV, and it was like he was talking to her directly. Gradually, she was able to eat, sleep, and function again with prayer and time. Prayer changes things.

My nursing supervisor had just lost her sister to breast cancer. She made a statement at the staff meeting that she, too, now had breast cancer. "It's not as aggressive as my sister's cancer was," she said with tears in her eyes. So, we were hopeful. After many prayers from the staff, she had a lumpectomy, then a mastectomy, and then chemotherapy. It was a long road, but God answered our prayers as well as her own, and she is cancer-free to this day. She is alive and well today—prayer matters.

My succeeding supervisor, I'll call her Tee, was the target of one mean individual who tried to gather all his followers against her to have her fired. This happened after he couldn't get to me because when He is for you, the forces of darkness will not prevail (Matthew 16:18).

God protected me from making an error in judgment or a medication error. That's when Tee removed me from that situation and gave me a new position. It was truly like Lucifer and his demons against God's people and angels. This went on for months. Everyone was praying for her, and my friend had her whole church praying for Tee. I soon bought Tee a Bible and showed her passages in the Bible to read, including Psalm 94, because darkness never covers the light, and good always prevails over evil. He eventually was found out for his lies, moved to another position, and let go. Prayer makes a difference.

I prayed all through my divorce to keep the house for my kids, to keep them in private school, to have enough money for all the things they needed. I prayed when my son asked for a leather jacket for school. He rarely asked for anything. So, out to Wilson's leather outlet we go, and he finds a jacket for $129, a size XL. I bought it for him as I wondered how I was going to make ends meet that month without the $129, as I was living paycheck to paycheck. I had no credit cards, no savings account. But I trusted that God would provide. Doesn't He care for the birds in the sky? Surely He would care for us. And as God always does, He provided. I received a check in the mail from DMV (Department of Motor Vehicles) refund check that week for $129! Prayer is love in action.

Another one of my patients, a woman in her late eighties, had brain cancer. She told me, "Laura, I had breast cancer in my 30s. I prayed my rosary every day to the Blessed virgin to stay alive and raise my children with my husband. I did the chemo, the radiation, and by the Grace of God, I beat cancer!" "Now," she said, "I am ok with dying. I am eighty-five years old; my children are all grown; my husband has died. My prayers have been answered." I was sent to ascertain why she refused all treatment. She calmly told me, "I do not want any more nausea, vomiting, diarrhea, hair loss, fatigue. I want to go naturally when it is my time. I'm ready to see my Lord." She wasn't depressed or psychotic. She was at peace with her decision, and I commended her for it. She reminded me of how prayers are answered and how she received a second chance at life.

## What is Prayer?
Prayer is love in its simplicity in your soul.
Prayer can be a simple thought, desire, or dream.
Prayer is a request,
Prayer is gratitude,
Prayer is grace,
Prayer is an acknowledgment,
Prayer is thanksgiving and praise,
Prayer is a conversation.
A one on one communication with God,

A personal relationship with the Father, the Son, and the Holy Spirit.

Our Father who art in heaven...
Our Father who art...
Our Father.

Thy Will Be Done...
Thy Will Be...
Thy Will.

When my friend Sue's mother became very ill and was spiraling downward, she was in the hospital, and then she returned home from the hospital, but my friend had to work. She knew she would have to hire someone to come in to help care for her mother. Being an aide herself, she knew how costly it might be. She prayed for an answer. Sue believes in giving to those in need. One day, she called the pastor, who started a Nursing Home. She called him to ask him what he needed. He told her he needed towels, sheets, washcloths, and she happily agreed to send whatever he needed. In conversation, she mentioned to him about her mother's condition. He said, "Your prayers are answered. Call this phone number." Sue immediately called the number, and a woman stated she would care for her mother five days a week for an affordable amount of money. Just because we cannot see a way, God makes a way!

I remember getting called to see a man who had prostate cancer for twenty years. When I first met him, he was in a hospital bed in the living room. He was pale, disheveled, just lying there, barely speaking. He managed to tell me his wife was working, and their daughter left for college. He was telling me how his appetite was nil and how weak he felt. I suggested he put some foods into the Nutribullet and make it like a smoothie so that it would be easier to drink rather than eat. He said he would try it.

I asked him about his faith and if it played a part in his twenty-year fight with cancer. He said, indeed, it had. He was grateful to God that He had allowed him to watch his kids grow up. The next time I saw him, he had gone into the city to his oncologist and had received a blood transfusion. The bed was gone, and he was sitting in a chair reading a book. He said he was a reader. His wife was present today. I told them as I was waiting in the car before I came in, I was reading Chapter 5 of Romans, which I thought pertained to him. The part where it says, "Not only that, but we even boast of our afflictions, knowing that affliction produces endurance, and endurance proven character, and proven character, hope, and hope does not disappoint because the love of God has been poured out into our hearts through the Holy Spirit that has been given to us" (Romans 5:3–5 NABRE).

I told him how great I thought he was for never giving up hope or his faith for the past twenty years! He told me that he was writing a book and I commended him on it. This was now his purpose for living and continuing all treatments and the hope of a cure. We parted ways with a God Bless you and keep you, and they thanked me for my visit. It was a confirmation that we all have trials and tribulations in this life, but trusting God is all the hope we will ever need.

Another patient of mine, a woman in her fifties, had ascites of the abdomen due to cancer that metastasized from the breast to the brain to the liver. She was alert and orientated. She was sitting in a recliner chair with edematous legs and abdomen. She was so full of life! But she, in fact, was dying and was in denial. She kept saying, "I'm getting better. I'm going to return to work soon." I measured her abdomen, and it measured 51 inches. She said, "I'm going to have a paracentesis done, and I'll be fine by next week." She thought she would return to work with the mentally handicapped. I could not crush this woman's hope. You just don't do that to someone because God can always turn it around. Nothing is impossible for Him.

Her son came home, and her daughter was there (studying to be a nurse) and also her husband. She had her faith and was relying on God to make her well again, never entertaining the thought if it were to be His will or not. The husband was very supportive, making her shakes or whatever she wanted. He was distraught. He walked outside with me and asked my opinion. I told him, "Honestly, I think hospice is in order here. But I dare not burst her bubble." That is something she and the family must talk about together and decide upon. He called me several times after that with questions, and I prayed and cried for her. Mostly for an answer because it wasn't in my hands anymore. It was in His hands now. The last call I received from him was, "Thank you, the hospice nurse came by today, and my wife accepted care at home."

This was when I realized, "Lord, it's not my job to heal them. It's my job to just love them."

Another family I remember well. She had a scarf on her head because of her baldness. Chemotherapy and radiation had taken its toll. She was slender and pale looking. She had cancer. Her children were in Catholic school, and she was involved with Smile Train, a well-known charity. She was involved in the PTA and had a very supportive husband and friends from her children's school and church members who brought food by. We discussed faith and how we heard about the God Squad, Jesus Christ Superstar, Godspell, folk masses (we were dating ourselves). She was full of life, not depressed, and clearly, she wanted to live.

I asked her, "Do you ever ask God, why me?"

She said, "No, I do ask God, why them?"

"Why who?" I asked.

She said, "The innocent children who get cancer."

I found this remarkable, the faith she had not to question her own illness but to question others! She said that she enjoyed the visit, and I told her I would pray for her, and I never saw her again. I was told by another nurse that she has been going through this for over a year now, and while the prognosis was not good, she was. This confirmed my assessment. She was living her life to the fullest, each and every day, a miracle in itself. This prompted me to write about how short our time on earth may actually be. While we take it for granted, it could be taken away in a blink of an eye.

In September of 2014, I wrote:

*Time... you can't get more of it like you can money.*

*Time... don't waste it like you can money.*

*Time... hold onto the memories because it is more precious than money.*

*Time... you cannot get it back (as you can money), so giving of your time is priceless.*

*Take time to smell the roses,*

*Take time to be with your children,*

*Take time to be with your family and friends,*

*Take time to love and laugh,*
*Take time to show others you care,*
*Take time to read and wonder,*
*Take time to pray and praise.*

St. Paul said to pray unceasingly. Prayer heals. Pray with all thanksgiving and gratitude and praise and worship in supplication with humility and boldness.

Prayer opens the very doors of the locked ones of our souls in which the key has long been lost.

Prayer is free. Free to say aloud or from within the depths of your very soul.

*Dare to Pray...*
*Dare to await the miracle.*

# CHAPTER 3

# God Incidents

"There is no such thing as co-incidents," as my sister, Christine, would always say, "For Christians, they are called God incidents." Those little things that happen that remind us that God is present; He is in charge. I've had many such incidents, and I'd like to share them with you. God does things for a reason, sometimes an answer to our prayers or His will. And sometimes we do not know why He does the things He does.

Richard's sister, Kim, who was still in Haiti, whom God finally got to a safe haven at the orphanage, with Mother Superior, who just happened to be in the next bed at the hospital where Rose was working—That's not a co-incident. Neither is this. Fast forward ten years later. Richard helped care for his grandmother with feeding and personal hygiene. Now, my mother is unable to care for herself and is in a nursing home. Now Richard has become a health aide himself and finds a job in a nursing home. Who do you think is assigned to my mother? Yes, it's Richard. God works in mysterious ways!

Another time, in 2014, my son Ronnie and I were planning a trip to Ireland together. He wanted to go because he never had the chance to go on a senior trip. It would be the first time I would be abroad with just myself and my twenty-five-year-old son. I prayed about this, and as usual, I ask God for a sign that it is the right thing to do. That same week during my home visits to the sick, I met not one but three women born in Ireland! That was my sign. I hadn't met one person from Ireland prior to this. We spoke about Ireland and from what town they were from and what town my mother's grandmother came from and to what towns we would be visiting. The number three is powerful—Father,

Son, and Holy Spirit. This confirmed for me that my trip would be blessed. And it was.

When I was out of work for five months, fear of losing the house, falling behind in the mortgage payment of $2,000 per month, living day to day trusting God would provide. Then, just when I felt I couldn't survive another thing, the washing machine breaks and water is pouring out all over the living room and bedroom floors. I was like, "God, You really want me to lose my mind altogether?" But after wiping up the rooms with towels, someone suggested I call the insurance company, which I did. They sent men with big blowers to prevent mold and dry up the area. The best thing was that the appraiser said that it was about $2,000 in damage for new flooring. I immediately cashed the check and paid my mortgage with the money. So, what tuned out looking like a bad situation, God turned it out for my good.

There have been several other occasions where God incident replaces co-incidents. The time I went to see a patient, and she wasn't home. Her husband pulled into the driveway as I arrived at the address I was given. He said, "She isn't here," and told me where she was. I met with her, and we talked about Joel Osteen and Joyce Meyers, and she said, "God sent you to me today." I felt overwhelming joy and confirmation that I was doing the Lord's work.

Another time my friend, Tee, was stuck at the airport for twelve hours during a snowstorm, and the plane landed in Pennsylvania instead of New York. She couldn't get home. Her daughter told her to rent a car, but she could not find her way home without a GPS, especially in the dark. She could only be on standby for the next flight to N.Y. She told me she said, "God, I'm leaving it up to you." She got the last seat on standby for N.Y. Never underestimate the power of prayer!

I remember a man who had CHF (congestive heart failure) refused to go to the hospital. If a patient is alert and coherent, and he refuses the Emergency Medical Service (EMS) team, they cannot force the patient to go. He was swollen and wheezing, and I was afraid he would not make it through the night. I prayed for him through the night to make it. The next day I drove over there because I had forgotten a folder, and it was a good excuse to check up on him. Upon arrival, the aide told me she was driving him to the Emergency Room (ER). I was told later he was admitted. I thanked God; he made it to the hospital. The Lord hears our prayers.

When my brother, who lived upstate, was going through a divorce, he wanted to take his three children to a water park. But he did not have the money to do so. He forgot about it. He remained faithful to the Lord. The very next week, a co-worker gave him four tickets to that same park, so he was able to take his kids! He called me to tell me. How awesome is our God? God knows the secrets of your heart. That's not a co-incident.

I can't remember what the medical diagnosis was of this man I was called to see, but I do remember him. He had two daughters, but he told me he had lost his faith when he lost his wife. I asked him, "How did she die?" He said, "I lost my wife to AIDS in 1991 from a blood transfusion after a hysterectomy." I told him how sorry I was for his loss, and he opened up a little and spoke about her. Before I left, I told him, "It's ok. I have enough faith for both of us." A tear came to his eye, and he said, "That's what she (my wife) used to say to me." I did not know that. How odd I would say that? All I can say is that God works through me, in me, and with me.

I then felt compelled to write:

**One Nurse's Prayer**
*Lord,*
*Let my hands help them,*
*Let my Eyes see their suffering,*
*Let my Ears hear what they cannot say,*
*Let my Voice console them,*
*Let my Mind teach them,*
*Let my Arms reach them,*
*Let my Heart love them, and Never*
*Let me Forget that they are All Your children,*
*Lord.*

My friend always asked before he went upstairs to the cafeteria, "Does anyone want coffee?" Two nurses said, "Yes." He told me, "I wanted a cup of coffee, but I only had enough for the two employees." He felt some change in his pocket. He had enough to buy a Lotto ticket, and he won $100! God rewarded him for denying himself and giving to others. He said he came back with breakfast for the other two employees and coffee for himself. I said to him, "God is good!" "All the time," he said. The more you are aware of God in everyday life, the more He shows up.

One day, my oldest brother said to me, "Have you ever looked up yourself on the internet?" I said, "No." He said, "I have. It's surprising what information about you is out there." Shortly after that, I decided to evangelize through the writing of a book. I felt God gently nudging me to do this, including retiring from my homecare nursing job. So, out of curiosity, I decided to lookup Laura Taggart. To my surprise, there was a picture of a woman about my age with blond hair, married with two grown sons. She is an established famous Christian author on the West Coast with a master's degree in theology. She founded a marriage counseling ministry in California. I am a blonde woman with two grown sons seeking to become an established Christian author on the East Coast. This was the "Go Ahead" from the Lord that I was seeking to write this book. My brother was amazed at this. Was this a co-incident or a God-incident?

Another time, I was sitting in church at the shrine of Our Lady. It was winter, and it was unusually cold out with snow pending. Father R. had just begun mass. In walked this disheveled looking man with black hair, black boots, black leather jacket, and dirty, ripped pants, mumbling to himself. All eyes were upon him. Where do you think he sat? Right next to me! He appeared to be schizophrenic because he talked to himself incoherently, sometimes loudly all through the mass. Father R. was giving me looks. He had a hundred other places to sit, but he chose the one next to probably the only psychiatric nurse in the whole church. As I got up for communion, he also did. I kept thinking, Lord, he is one of yours, and I will treat him that way.

Didn't Jesus say to give to the least of my brothers? And aren't the mentally ill the outcast in society? When mass was over, I asked him if he was hungry, and he said, "I could use a cup of coffee." I handed him some money and told him there was a cafeteria here, and they sell food. He said, "Thank you," and walked away. I believe God puts us in the right place at the right time for a reason!

One time, my mother was in the hospital, and she was going in and out of consciousness. I said to my brother, "I think she has water on her brain again." She had hydrocephalus and had a shunt put in her head several years ago. I surmised that the shunt was not working correctly. I was working but managed to get off early to get to the hospital to speak to the doctor in charge of her and make her aware of my thoughts. My mother had all the symptoms, and my youngest brother said, "I googled it, and yes, she has all the symptoms." Confusion, increased urination, headache, unsteady gait, and I made the doctor aware of them all, but she completely dismissed me like I was a nobody. She would not do a single test to confirm. No matter what I said to her, she refused. I said, "Lord, she (doctor) is willing to let her die than to do the necessary tests. Please give me the inclination of what I should do." I went to the hospital with my two brothers, and I prepared them that I will take this over her head to the administration.

I called the neurosurgeon from another hospital who did the original surgery and explained to him the symptoms my mother was having and how we, my brothers and I, were not willing to let her die. He said, "I'll be right there." He came right over, and I assisted him in taking four tubes of cerebral spinal fluid off of her brain right in her room! He then said, "She will recover; it may take a day or so." I thanked him profusely, and he left the room. With that, my mother sat up and began speaking! I ran out to the nurses' desk and said to him, "It's a miracle! She's awake and talking!" She was later transferred back to the original hospital, where a newer shunt was placed. Wasn't that a God incident that Dr .G. wasn't in surgery and was able to come right away to another hospital? God still works miracles today.

I was having some health issues during my last job and didn't want to work part-time, but just one or two days a week. I said, "Lord, I'm not a quitter. You will let me know when enough is enough." On one particular day, I was visiting an Eighty-five-year-old lady, and we had a good rapport. She noticed that I was having difficulty getting up her steps with my work bag and my computer. She said, "Are you ok?" I said, "Yes, I'm just getting old, I guess." And we laughed. Later she said, "Laura, you should really stop taking care of me because in doing so, you're only hurting yourself." That's when it hit me; she was right. It's like I had confirmation that I wasn't a quitter, I just physically couldn't do this job anymore, and it was God's way of letting me know.

That's when I felt like God is asking me to "trust Him" and put it into action. This has been one of the hardest things for me to do. To surrender all and give God control and to trust Him, I will have enough money and will not go crazy staying home. I cannot drive for hours anymore. I cannot walk in the snow or go up the stairs with my heavy work bag. I felt a weight taken off my shoulders when I told my boss C (because I felt she was pushing me out the door anyway). I really don't need the money, it was never about the money anyway, although it was nice to have. I'll live on my pension from the state of N.Y. Maybe, so I don't get bored, I could work one day a week to help people or volunteer somewhere.

When I decided to put in an application to another hospital, I was sure to get the job. With my friend Tee's letter of recommendation, as she used to be the nurse manager there, and I knew the head of education there... but I didn't. The nurse recruiter called two weeks later, woke me up, and said in a cheery voice, "Good Morning Laura, this is the nurse recruiter from such-n-such hospital; how are you?" I said, "Good, good." She then said, "I'm sorry we do not have a position available for you here, but good luck." And she hung up. I thought that was the weirdest phone call of all. But... sometimes, we do not understand how or why God does the things He does. My friend T. was very ill with stage 4 colon cancer, and now I would be able to take her to chemotherapy. God does things for a reason. This is where I would be needed now.

I started to research Mercy Ships and the Red Cross and was driving myself crazy with what God wanted me to do next with my life because if I wasn't working, I felt I had to volunteer somewhere to feel useful.

I said, "God, what do you want me to do now?"

He said, "Be Still and Know that I am God."

I felt He was saying, "Relax, I will let you know what, where, and when I want you to go."

Now, I learned I need double hip replacements, or I would never walk again. This was God again telling me loud and clear that I will not work now. I think He was telling me to write His book while I recovered from my hip surgeries. I was watching TBN when I saw the advertisement for the Trilogy publishing company. I called them to get an idea of what it would entail and spoke to Rhett, who was very encouraging. I remember hearing Matt and Laurie Crouch say, "To tell your story is evangelizing!" That's when it hit me. God had a project for me. He would write the book for me. I would once again be His instrument. I said, "Ok, God, this is different, I'm used to a one-on-one encounter, but if we can reach more people this way, and if only one person is transformed to believe in You, it will be all worth it." Everything happens in God's timing; I've come to learn.

Like the time I was in Tanzania, Africa, on a missionary trip, with my friend Loretta (whom I had just met) and her daughter Raeann, we visited schools and orphanages. We gave the books, crayons, school supplies, toys, clothes, and candy, which we brought with us for the many children. We assisted in pouring cement for a school. We saw where a church was to be built with our donations. It was a worthwhile, rewarding trip, and I highly recommend it. The people are warm and friendly. The smiles on the children's faces were priceless. You actually feel like you are making a difference.

We stayed at the Bishops' Epiphany house. There was M., who was Father F.'s brother, who was our driver and safari guide in our green off-road Range Rover. It was very nice and big with an open roof to enjoy picture taking of the safari animals. Wildebeests, zebras, monkeys, baboons, giraffes, elephants, hippos, lions all in the wild; it was a breathless experience.

M. drove us to and from the Serengeti safari. It was a long ride, and we were to stay at a convent for the night and continue to the Serengeti National park the next day. M. took a liking to me because I kept him awake, asking him questions about his country in the dark and perilous journey around the mountainside (with no guard rails or lights, except for the stars) to the convent, which we stayed the night before. A moped driver we met in town was to lead us up the steep mountainside. I was on the left where the edge was and was silently praying. The order of nuns was called *Daughters of Mary*, but of course! They had a beautiful dinner all ready for us with private rooms with running water and toilets, and beautiful gardens with fresh homegrown vegetables and flowers. The grounds were so beautiful; you would have thought you were in a little piece of heaven on earth.

While we were coming from our Serengeti safari after having an American dinner, it was so nice to have a drink and an American dinner for a change. We were staying at the Bishops' "Epiphany house," and the nuns there were preparing our food, but they did not cook any American dishes. There were five women, including myself and an older man named J.

As we were eating dinner, I overheard the chef at the restaurant say to M., how it may be dangerous traveling at night because of robbery and such! I asked M. about it, and he said, "We'll be ok. We have God on our side!" I said, "Ok."

During our travels, I asked him how much cows, goats, and chickens cost and which American songs he knew. I sang Tina Turner's song, *Rolling on the River* for him and *Rocky Mountain High* by John Denver. He also knew some of Elvis Presley's songs. So, with that being said, M. wanted me to sit in front with him on the way home too. It was a good thing I did!

Suddenly, we heard a thump, thump, thump. We had gotten a flat tire! Naturally, I got out to help him get the jack and the spare tire out to assist him in changing it. Loretta gave me a coal miner's light to put on my head, so M. could see what he was doing. It was pitch black out. I kept watching all around also so that no one could sneak up on us. One woman wanted to get out of the truck, so as to lighten the load for the manual jack, and both M. and I screamed, "NO" at the same time. That's all we would have needed for someone to see five helpless white, American women on the side of the road. That's like an invitation to rob us! Loretta's daughter Raeann said, "Well, if anyone, I'm glad Laura is out there with him." I would have put up a good fight if I had to.

After the tire was put on the truck, we are on the road again, and everyone breathed a sigh of relief. But not for long... We had been getting stopped at each town border by police or people pretending to be police. I said to M., "I will give you money to bribe them with." He looked at me and took the money and said, "Yes, this will help." No one else knew of our plan.

This was the scariest for me because they had on army fatigues and had machine guns, and we could not understand the language. I just looked out the window when we were stopped and prayed. This worked four out of the five times without a problem. I pretended to look the other way as to not let on to the "Officer" that M. was giving him money. This time M. strategically put the tire iron under his seat so that I could reach it if need be. At the last stop, the "officer" made M. get out of the vehicle and took him to the back of the truck! At that point, I didn't know if he was coming back. I prayed to Our Lady and Our Lord to show me what I needed to do next. The other women were also praying. I was preparing to get the tire iron when M. walked back to the drivers' side of the truck. I was ever so relieved that once again, "God was on our side," just as M. had said. I believe that God put me in that front seat for a reason.

It was a beautiful trip, and I encourage anyone to go on a missionary trip to Africa because all the orphanages, schools, churches, children, and people we visited were very nice and very appreciative of all we did for them. It was truly a once in a lifetime experience. Just ask Loretta's daughter, Raeann. She volunteered for a humanitarian organization in Tanzania, where she stayed with a host family for two months. She has been back three times and plans to return again this summer! My sister's nephew on her husband's side volunteered in Tanzania in the Peace Corps and loved it so much he signed up twice!

Have you ever felt God? You guessed it. Raeann has, and it was in Tanzania.

Loretta told me her daughter texted her, "I feel God."

Loretta's husband said, "She must have missed the other "o" for good."

Loretta texted her daughter, and she texted back, "No, I mean God."

Loretta said, "I want to hear this story; call me."

I asked Rae about the story, and here is what she told me.

We were coming back from safari, and we made a random stop at a tourist shop. I saw Jay talking to a man in a Harvard sweatshirt. Jay was telling the man about some of the children from one of the schools who needed surgery. The man was telling Jay that he was an archeologist, and it was his third or fourth trip when he injured his finger. He went to this hospital called "Fame" run by a couple from California, and they fixed his finger, or he would have lost it. When we got back into the truck, they had a new driver, not M. from last time.

They asked him if he knew where this hospital was, and he said he did. He took us to it because it was off the beaten path. We spoke to the doctors there of the ailments of the children, and I also mentioned that my host father had a problem with his rectum and leakage, and the doctors agreed to do surgery on them! When we got back, we asked M. if he knew where the hospital was, and he did not. He was sick that day and could not drive us to the safari.

Raeann said, "My host father's problem was cured, and one of the girls who couldn't walk can now walk! I felt that God was in the middle of all of this and made all of this happen. Only He could have orchestrated these series of events and the outcomes!"

I remember the day I had to put my dog, Simon, to sleep. He was a big furry Akita looking dog. He was the best dog ever! He was good at protecting you. He barked whenever anyone approached, never bit anyone, and he never had an accident in the house. He was my son, Jonathan's' dog, which now became my dog since Jonathan had moved to Chicago. He was with us for thirteen years. I had him on medication because his back had blown up with a tumor making it hard for him to walk, his eyes had cataracts, and now he walked all night like in some kind of dementia, not sleeping.

The vet put him on three different medications but to no avail. It was time, the vet said. I really had some reservations being that God gave life, was it my choice to take it away? Some say it was the humanitarian thing to do but was it? As I held him in my arms, I tearfully told him how much I loved him (My son Ronnie was with me. Thank God.), and I told him that Jesus loved him too. When I came home, I sat at my dining room table crying and thinking, *Please God, tell me that "All dogs go to heaven," and Lord, please tell me that he's walking with you.* All of a sudden, my photo projector came on, and pictures of all the animals in Africa came on (pictures that had never come up before) that I didn't even know were on the chip. The wildebeests, the elephants, the giraffes, the hippos, the monkeys, the baboons. I heard the Lord say, "I love all of my animals I have created." It made sense; otherwise, why would Noah have been bothered to put two of all the animals on the ark? I took it as a sign that my Simon was with the Lord.

Before my best friend Tee died after fighting colon cancer for two years, I was driving her to chemotherapy, and I was telling her of Roma Downey's new book, which I had just read, *Box of Butterflies*. She told me she was "afraid to die". She said that she told her children that when she died, if she made it to heaven, she would send them a sign, a butterfly. I just said, "OK." When she did die, my friend, Renuka, drove me to the funeral because I had just had surgery on my left hip and could not drive. She was on vacation and had just returned from Costa Rica, and she didn't know what Tee had told me. She brought me back a towel and earrings. I half-heartedly looked at them because after coming from the funeral mass, I was a mess. I thanked my friend and went into my room to cry. I then remembered what Tee had said about sending a butterfly. Didn't that towel have the biggest, bluest butterfly on it? That couldn't be a coincidence. Being that it was January and there are no real butterflies around, it was Tee's sign that she was in heaven after all. I called her daughter and my friend

Renuka to tell them. I felt relieved. The next morning when I awoke, I heard in my heart, "Laura, you were right. It's really not that bad here." It was God's way of letting me know she was "OK" and that she was with Him.

Just recently, I went to my dentist of thirty years between surgeries for a cleaning. Oddly enough, I overheard another patient say, "I can't believe it's your last day."

I said, "I heard it's your last day?"

He said, "Yes, didn't you get the letter?"

I answered, "What letter?"

He said, "I sent out a letter stating this and who will be covering for me."

I told him, "I never received a letter."

I asked, "Are you moving?"

He said, "No, I'm retiring."

I knew him as a surfer dude in his prime and thought he was moving to Florida. He had also been to Africa on a missionary trip and fixed teeth there for free. I knew him as a good dude.

He said, "I'm going to be a mussel farmer."

I said, "Okay, how did that come about?"

He said, "I volunteered one day and found I loved it."

I told him of my writing a book called, Live outside the box, and he went on to tell me how mussels clean the water, are good for the environment, they are good to eat, and there is money to be made. He told me how his wife couldn't wait for the demolition of his offices (in their home).

He also said, "I'm out in the fresh air, in the water, in the sun, it's like..."

"Heaven," I said for him.

He smiled shyly and said, "Yeah."

I do not think that I was there on his last day as a dentist as a coincidence. Here was a man truly putting it all out there and trusting God to make a way for him. He had more faith than I gave him credit for.

It's like the actor Jim Caviezel was saying, that "It's not a coincidence that I was thirty-three-years-old and my initials are J.C. and that Mel Gibson found me to play "Jesus" in *The Passion of the Christ* movie." Jim's shoulder separated while carrying the cross and how it made him fall to his knees, and it was filmed that way. He said that he felt he was unworthy of playing the part. He prayed a lot of the time. He said he heard a voice telling him he was going to die today, which he thought to be the devil. He goes on to say it was a life-changing experience for him where he was ready to die for Christ and almost did die on that cross. Then he was literally hit by lightning, and the ground shook. He suffered from pneumonia while hanging on the cross, and he had to have heart surgery afterward.[14] Just watch any of his videos on YouTube. He has an inspiring message for all. He then went on to play Luke in Paul the *Apostle of Christ* movie, and he did a phenomenal job there too. God is always faithful.

I remember I went to a friend's daughter's baby shower, and at my table sat a nun. I asked her, "Is your name Mary Ellen?" She said, "No, that is the name I chose, but they gave me the name Sister Phyllis instead." I wondered what on earth made me say that? It had to be the Holy Spirit, although I did not realize it at the time.

Recently my sister, Christine, called me to tell me that she got the job that we were all praying that she would get working with disabled veterans and driving them places that she gets to pick out. She said it is $1.00 more an hour, and now she is not entitled to the HEAP program for money for heat. She said she wasn't going to try to gyp God. God doesn't like that. But this is how my God works. She said when she got a check in the mail for $249, she called them to tell them she is not eligible for the money any longer because of the raise in salary. They told her it is not from HEAP; it is extra money in the budget for the summer's air conditioning

14 "The Passion of The Christ - Jim Caviezel (Complete Interview)." 2013. Catholic Inside USA YouTube. 2020. https://www.youtube.com/channel/UCE1gMy-ucEoA7C5TtBN0PPg.

bill, which she was entitled to because she just got the job two weeks ago.

It was after Mass at the shrine that a psychologist was to speak, and it was Pentecost Sunday. Usually, I don't stick around, but today I felt compelled to stay and listen since he was in my field of work. He, the doctor, spoke about the Trinity and how the Holy Spirit is always with us. He had two other women with him, and after his talk, he said, "If anyone would like laying on of hands with the Holy Spirit to form a line one at a time." I thought maybe I could ask for healing for my sister, who has a weak immune system and is always sick from the daycare kids she teaches. So, I waited in line, and when it was my turn, I said, "I'm not here for myself; I'm here for my sister." With that, one lady placed her hands on my head and said,

"OH, I feel the Holy Spirit here."

I explained about my sister and that I was intrigued by his teaching being that I am a psychiatric nurse myself.

He said, "Those psychiatric nurses were so good to my son. He was a schizophrenic, and he eventually committed suicide."

I said, "I'm so sorry."

He said to me, "Don't ever think that your job is insignificant because they cannot thank you. You are doing the Lord's work."

And with that, he gave me a big hug and said, "Yes, we will pray for your sister's healing."

When Ronnie decided to go hiking on a mountain in the winter to see a waterfall, I asked him to take some pictures for my book. He had never been here before. I was waiting in the car for him. About five hours later, I started to pray. I could not get him on his phone (no reception), and I had a bad feeling about this. I asked that God send his guardian angel to protect him so he would not get lost or fall off the mountain in the snow. I now stood in the road and began screaming his name. When he did return, he said it was very treacherous, and he slipped on the snow a couple of times. There was a sign that said people have fallen off this mountain under good conditions. When he showed me the picture of the frozen waterfall, I said, "That's a picture of an angel."

One day I was praying to God about sending me a sign (I always do this) to move after thirty years in the same house to Palm Coast, Florida. Over the summer, the priest gave a sermon about St. Augustine, which is one town away from Palm Coast. Then I saw a kid with a St. Augustine, Florida t-shirt on at the beach concert I went to. But it wasn't enough. On my way to physical therapy in the fall, I was waiting for a lady who was talking to the receptionist (her back towards me), and she says to them, my neurologist said, "He's going to have to fax over a book," referring to her records. She then said, "It's Jacksonville, St. Augustine, and then I couldn't hear anymore. Her back was to me, so I didn't notice what she looked like. After she left, I anxiously asked the receptionist,

"Is she moving to Florida?"

She said, "Yes."

I said, "Palm Coast?"

She said, "Yes."

I said, "Oh, I'm thinking of moving there myself."

Coincidence, I think not. The next day of my physical therapy, I see a woman waiting behind me in line, and I intuitively turned around and said,

"Are you the lady moving to Palm Coast?"

She said, "Yes, I bought a house."

I said, "Oh, I want to buy too, but I have to sell my house first."

She said, "Me too, but the seller is willing to wait for me."

I said, "Ok."

What are the chances of all the people, in all the days, in all the hours and minutes of a day, moving to the same place as you? And not once but twice. I'd say that was God speaking loud and clear that it was ok to move to Palm Coast. A few days later, I awoke and heard, "Finish MY book." It has to be on His time, not mine, and apparently, He wants His book finished first.

# Super Heroes

Everyone has a favorite superhero—Whether it is Batman, Superman, Spiderman, Wonder Woman, or any of the Marvel comic book superheroes. Mine doesn't fly, leap tall buildings in a single bound, stick to buildings with a web, or round up the bad guys. Mine hears prayers, makes miracles happen, rises from the dead, and loves with an everlasting love.

Mine is the Trinity—Father, Son, and Holy Spirit. Three persons in one true God. Just like water is a liquid (water), solid (ice), and a gas (water vapor). All with different characteristics, yet the same basic thing, water.

God, the Father, is both Jesus' father and our father too. God created heaven and earth all the creatures, water, land, trees, stars, and man and woman (Genesis 2:4, 7, 22). He created it all for man to rule over, and when He finished what He had done, He found it very good (Genesis 1:31). God is Love. He loves us. God is good, all the time. As one pastor put it, Good stands for God overcoming obstacles daily.

It was God who told Noah to build an ark and take two of every animal into it with him and his family (Genesis 6:14, 7:7). For forty days and nights it rained, and all of creation was destroyed (Genesis 7:17, 23). God then promised Noah that He would never again destroy the earth with water and gave a rainbow as the sign between Him and the earth (Genesis 9:13). God also spared Abraham from sacrificing his only son Isaac, on the altar so that He would send His only Son down to earth to die in order to redeem us from our sins (Genesis 22:12; John 3:16). The same God led Moses to bring His people out of slavery from the land of Egypt (Exodus 12:42). The Lord God parted the Red Sea, and all the Israelites passed through, and when Pharaoh's army passed through, the Sea swallowed them up, drowning all of them (Exodus 14:27, 28). It was in the desert that He provided for them (Exodus 16:13). Here, He spoke to Moses, giving him the Ten Commandments for all men (Exodus 20:2). God told Joshua to have His people walk around the walls of Jericho in silence except for the seven priests marching with the ark of the Lord, blowing the ram's horn (Joshua 6:7, 10, 14). They did this for six days. On the seventh day, Joshua's people marched around six times as they had previously done, but on the seventh time around, they were shouting and blowing the ram's horn, and the walls came tumbling down (Joshua 6:15). Only Rahab and her family were saved because she had saved Joshua's spies from their enemies by hiding them on the roof of her house (Joshua 6:17).

It was God who gave Manoah's wife a child, even though she was barren (Judges 13:2). A son named Samson, who found favor with the Lord and was given superhuman strength (Judges 13:24). He killed one thousand Philistines with just a jawbone of an ass, and God split the cavity in Lehi and water issued from it so Samson could drink and be revived (Judges 15:15, 19). When Delilah found out the source of Samson's strength was in his hair, she had his head shaved and handed him over to the Philistines (Judges 16:19). They gouged out his eyes (Judges 16:21). But his hair grew back, and God gave him the strength back, and he took down two columns in the temple of the Philistines where Samson killed approximately three thousand people, including himself (Judges 16:22, 30). God guided a Jewish girl, Esther, to the king in order to save her people from destruction. With her beauty and courage, she won favor from king Ahasuerus and was made Queen, and then saved her people from annihilation (Esther 2:17, 7:7, 8). It was God who gave Elizabeth, Mary's cousin, a child, a son long after she was of childbearing age named John the Baptist (Luke 1:36, 60). And it was God who sent an angel to announce to a virgin named Mary that she would become the mother of God and bear a Son named Jesus (Luke 1:31). It was a loving God who loved the world so much that He sent his only Begotten Son (John 3:16). God is a loving God!

You can trust Him. God loves you. He knows everything about you. He knew you before you were born (Psalm 139:13). He knows the number of hairs on your head (Luke 12:7). He answers prayers too. He still sends the Holy Spirit to guide and speak to us. He still has His angels watching over us. And yes, He can do miracles, even today. He answers prayers too. He makes things happen for a reason, not just a coincidence. He has blessings stored up for you right here on earth. He is Almighty God. He has a heaven awaiting you when you die. He even has a manual called the Bible.

On Eternal Word Network (EWTN), I heard Father Cedric once say, "Bible stands for Basic Info Before Leaving Earth."[15]

As it is written,

*And we know that all things work for good to those who love God, who are called according to his purpose.*

(Romans 8:28 NKJV)

Also,

*"For I know the plans I have for you," declares the Lord, "plans to prosper you and not to harm you plans to give you hope and a future."*

(Jeremiah 29:11 NIV)

So, don't put God in a box, on a shelf for a rainy day. Read the Bible, if only a verse a day. It's easy; you can even get an app on your phone. God has good things in store for you if you only Believe...

---

15 "Father Cedric Pisegna Ministries—Houston Texas." 2006. Www.Frcedric.Org. 2006. https://frcedric.org/default.aspx?MenuItemID=174&MenuGroup=Public+Home.

I remember one night returning from Chicago. My youngest son, Jonathan, was attending Loyola University, and my friend Amber and I were picking him up for summer break from his dorm. It was a thirteen-hour drive from Chicago back to Long Island, New York. I was driving and coming up on the hour eight or ten, and I was getting sleepy. I had suggested that maybe we rent a room for the night so that I could get some sleep. They did not think that was a good idea because of the area we were in. I stopped at a gas station to ask where we were and how much further to N.Y. The man stated that we were in Pennsylvania and had about five more hours to go and that there were no motels close by. So, I started to pray. I prayed that God would get us safely home. I prayed the "Our Father" (Luke 11:2–4 NKJV).

It was approximately 2 a.m., pitch black outside, no lights except for my headlights on the highway, and my eyes were starting to close, but blinking helped open them again. Out of nowhere comes a pickup truck ahead of me. I said, "Oh, thank you, God, you've sent me an angel to light the way!" At least, I had light from his tail lights and could follow him through the winding roads. This worked out well for a while. Suddenly, a piece of metal flew up towards the windshield, startling me; I screamed. That awakened both my son and my friend. As I slowed down, I saw two tractor-trailers hit one another, and the guy in the pickup truck pulled over. I later pulled over to see if there was any damage to my truck, but there was none, not a scratch on the car. Amber said, "We could have been killed!" But when I told her I was praying when that happened, she said, "He was watching out for us."

When I was on a cruise ship in the middle of the ocean, I was just contemplating how marvelous our God really is, and I wrote:

*God's Loves is as vast as the*
*Depth of the ocean.*
*God's mercies are as countless*
*As the drops of water in the sea.*
*God's graces are as many as*
*The number of waves in the ocean.*
*And God's blessings are as endless as*
*The ebb and flow of the tides.*

Jesus, who is also both God and man, was foretold by the prophets centuries before He came to the earth. He was real. History accounts for His birth and death and life in Nazareth as a carpenter/craftsman. He was humbly born in Bethlehem to a virgin named Mary (Luke 2:4–7). Jesus came for all men, both Jews and Gentiles. This was proven when the Magi came from far off lands in the East because they saw the star over Bethlehem

(Matthew 2:2). The Wisemen knew the Messiah had come for them as well as the Jews, and they came to bring Him gifts and to worship Him (Matthew 2:11).

Jesus was beaten and crucified for us to redeem us from our sins and teach us the meaning of forgiveness (Luke 23:33, 34). He prayed, in the Garden of Gethsemane, "My Father, if it is possible, let this cup pass from me; yet, not as I will but as you will," not once, but three times He asked (Matthew 26:39 NASB). It was not God's will. He had the choice of following God's will for His life or not. He had legions of angels at His beck and call at any given moment who could have taken Him off that cross, but He knew that was not how the scripture was to be fulfilled (Matthew 26:53). He could have said, "Hey, being the sacrificial lamb is not for me. Why am I my brother's keeper?" Love kept Him on the cross. He knew that it was the only way we would be saved and that it was His Father's will. Just as Jesus taught us to pray, "Your will be done on earth as it is in heaven" (Matthew 6:10 NKJV). He also said, "...Father, forgive them; for they know not what they do" (Luke 23:34 KJV). Then Jesus was buried and rose from the dead on the third day, and before ascending into heaven, He appeared to many (Luke 4:46, 24:51; Acts 1:3). I think this is the best superpower I've ever seen.

His name is Jesus Christ, sent by God the Father for our salvation. His followers are called Christians. While

He was on earth, He worked miracles. He made blind men see, the deaf to hear, the lame to walk (Mark 8:23–25, 8:34–35, 2:11). He also cured the sick and the lepers, drove out demons, turned five loaves of bread and two fishes into enough food to feed thousands (Mark 1:31, 41–42, 1:25, 6:41–42). He even walked on water! (Luke 6:19). He turned water into wine and raised Lazarus up from the dead (John 7:7–9, 11:44). Talk about Living Outside the Box... He came to preach to us about how we should and should not live while on this earth and about the reward of living forever in heaven with God.

The best part is that Jesus came for all of us and can be our superhero, not just mine alone. It just takes a little faith (Faith of a mustard seed). It reminds me of a story I read a long time ago, a short story by Paul Harvey, titled, The Man and the Birds, about a man who saw birds fly right into his lit, landscape window during a snowstorm, and died as they hit the glass. He thought that if he put a light on in the barn with a trail of breadcrumbs, they would fly in there instead of the window where they would be safe. But the birds were too afraid to go into the barn, so they kept flying into the glass and dying. Then the farmer thought, if only I could be a bird... so then they could see, hear, and understand and follow me, and I could show them the way. That is how he realized why Jesus had to come to earth as a man.[16]

I was sent to see a woman with pulmonary hypertension. She lived with her two daughters, son, and a two-year-old granddaughter. She was on oxygen twenty-four hours a day, seven days a week. She also had two very big protective pit bulls. Her daughters had to put the dogs behind a locked door when anyone came to visit. As I spoke to her, she tearfully told me that she was losing her house. She was very anxious about this because she had pictures that she showed me of how she built the house from the ground up. She was calling the mortgage company and the bank trying to stop the foreclosure. We talked about her faith. I explained to her that sometimes God calls us to "let go" of material things and that her health was my primary concern right now.

The insurance company would not allow another visit, so I called her on my vacation, and she told me that her son told her that "He will build me a bigger and better house," and she was able to let go of the worry and anxiety, which had improved her breathing. As I was leaving the house, one of the big dogs got loose and came running and barking at me. I froze, put the com-

16 "Paul Harvey and 'The Man and the Birds.' Posted 2019." 2020. Christian Heritage Fellowship, Inc. 2020. https://christianheritage-fellowship.com/paul-harvey-and-the-man-and-the-birds/.

puter up to my face, and screamed, "Jesus." Just as the dog was going to jump on me, he stopped and turned around. I said, "Thank you, God," and never quite realized the power in the name of Jesus as I had that day.

To *Live Outside the Box* like Jesus did, knowing that anything is possible with a little faith, is awesome—to *dream, imagine, believe, trust,* and *love.* My Jesus hears and answers my prayers. He knows what I am going through when I'm going through it. He sometimes helps me out of it or allows me to grow through it with the Holy Spirit's guidance, allowing me to make it through to the other side.

Having been both human and divine, Jesus knows what we are feeling. He knows what it's like. He gets it. He's experienced hurt, anger, betrayal, abandonment, pain, and suffering. But He's also experienced love, joy, friendship, compassion, and peace.

People don't deny that Jesus walked the earth and performed miracles. Some think He was a nice guy or a great teacher or a prophet. No, Jesus clearly states that He is the Son of God, which is the Messiah who was foretold centuries beforehand (Jeremiah 23:5–6). Jesus gave us the two greatest commandments:

*...You shall love the Lord your God with all your heart, with all your soul, and with all your mind. This is the greatest and the first commandment.*

(Matthew 22:37–38 NABRE)

He preached,

*This is My commandment, that you love one another as I have loved you. Greater love has no one than this, than to lay down one's life for his friends.*

(John 15:12–13 NKJV)

But Jesus was too radical (as stated by Matthew Kelly) for many.[17] For others He was just too humble a person and did not become the great king that they had imagined.

A long time ago, an email went around with this poem, written by Lyle C. Rollings III in 2006; it was about Jesus.

The Greatest Man in History

The greatest man in history... Jesus had no servants, yet they called Him Master.

Had no degree, yet they called Him Teacher.

Had no medicines, yet they called Him Healer.

He had no army, yet Kings feared Him.

He won no military battles, yet He Conquered the world.

---

17 Kelly, Matthew. 2015. Rediscover Jesus: An Invitation. Beacon Publishing. https://www.goodreads.com/book/show/27968974-rediscover-jesus.

He did not live in a castle, yet they called Him Lord,

He ruled no nations, yet they called Him King,

Committed no crime, yet they crucified Him.

He was buried in a tomb yet He lives today.

I feel honored to serve such a Leader who loves us![18]

According to C.S. Lewis in his book *Mere Christianity* he writes:

A man who was merely a man and said the sort of things Jesus said would not be a great moral teacher. He would either be a lunatic-on the level with a man who says he is a poached egg- or he would be the devil of hell. You must take your choice. Either this was, and is , the Son of God, or else a madman or something worse. You can shut him up for a fool or you can fall at his feet and call him Lord and God. But let us not come with any patronizing nonsense about his being a great

---

18 "The Greatest Man in History - A Poem by Lyle C. Rollings III, 2007." 2017. All Poetry. 2017.

human teacher. He has not left that open to
us.[19]

He's also the only man today that is still spoken
about, written about, wondered about, for over 2,000
years.

The Holy Ghost or the Holy Spirit is the third person
in the Holy Trinity. I was under the misconception that
the Holy Spirit was a dove. It was said that the Spirit
descended upon Jesus like a dove while John the Baptist
was baptizing him (Mark 1:10). But later, I read that the
Holy Spirit descended upon the apostles and all those
gathered together on Pentecost Sunday as a tongue of
fire above their heads. Thus, giving them the ability to
speak in different tongues, as the Spirit enabled them
to proclaim. There were devout Jews from every nation
present, and each one all heard the Galileans speak in
their native language (Acts 2:3–11).

The Holy Spirit still speaks today. Sometimes it is
in a dream, a thought, or a whisper. Today, the Holy
Spirit also speaks to God's people in "tongues". A language between only God and the few elect who can interpret. My friend Renuka discovered that she had the
gift of tongues when she experienced it for herself in a
church she was visiting. She thought, as many did, that

---

19  Lewis, C. S. 2001. *Mere Christianity*. New York, NY: Harper
Collins, 227.

those things were staged, and the pastor had set that person up prior to the service to talk like that. She said she didn't know what she was saying but that it was her voice. Another parishioner interpreted her message for the church.

Recently, the Holy Spirit whispered to me, "Get Her a Phone." My sister Christine had an old flip phone that you pay for minutes. She never had any reception at her home. One day she called me to tell me she had a blood pressure reading of 198/110. I told her I was concerned because that is what I call "stroke time". She said her job had caught it and told her to rest until it came down, return to work, and leave work at the usual time. Now, I was worried because I felt she should have been sent to the emergency room for follow up. Now, she went home, lives alone, and cannot even call for help. Now, I was upset because I didn't know if she would make it through the night!

I did what I do when I don't know what else to do, I pray. That is when it hit me, "Get her a phone" like a whisper, so simple. I immediately went to Verizon and explained the situation to the girl behind the counter. Of course, she did her sales pitch first. "Buy the new Samsung 10 phone and get another for free," she said. But I explained to her that would be too expensive of an option for me. So, she then said, "Well, if you only want to add another phone line to your three existing ones, we can give you a free phone!" I said, "I'll take it!" For $19.99 a month, I would have peace of mind that my sister could call for help in case of an emergency; it was well worth it. She, Lorraine, was so nice she made my sister a google account, and she put the Holy Bible and the daily bread apps on her phone for her. Now tell me that God did not have a hand in that! I just paid the tax on it.

I told my sister, "I'm sending a package to you as your birthday present."

She said, "That's odd, a month in advance?"

I said, "Yes," without telling her what it was. When she received it, she accepted it, realizing it was necessary.

Another time, the Holy Spirit led me to go to Pennsylvania, get my eighty-year-old mother, who is in a wheelchair, to see her dying brother with my cousin to see his dying father. I knew that only by the grace of God would He get me there and back safely for this four-hour drive each way and give me the strength to accomplish it. God sent us an angel called George, the Intensive Care Unit Registered Nurse (ICU RN). He looked up my uncles' name and found his son, my cousin, with the same name only with Jr. after it on the computer. He had been estranged from his father for approximately ten years. I spoke to the nurse, after explaining who I was, and he said that his liver and kidneys are failing and that my uncle would not make it until next weekend.

It was snowing quite heavily, and my cousin arrived approximately three hours before we did and made amends with his father. My uncles' mind was alert and orientated. He now wanted to leave his money, house, truck, and camper to his only son. The only problem was that my uncle had left it all to me, except his money, which he left to his lawyer's daughter. I told my cousin, "I do not want any of his things; they belong to you, you are his son, and I will gladly sign them over to you." It was late Saturday night, and it was unlikely my uncle could get the lawyer to change the will on a Sunday. That night, I prayed and prayed that things would go well for my uncle and my cousin. All of a sudden, my mother, while asleep, sits up in bed, points directly at me, and states, "You're next!" I quickly called my friend, Amber, who has the gift of discernment, and she stated that "an evil spirit must have been in the room." She said, "Quick, look in the draw for a Bible, all hotels have them, read Psalm 91 out loud, and bind Satan in the name of Jesus." At the very moment, I finished the psalm, with tears in my eyes, my mother awoke. She said, "I must have been dreaming," and did not say another word the whole night. There is power in prayer. I was up until 4 a.m. praying.

When we got up to go back to the hospital the next morning, the nurse said that my uncle did not sleep hardly at all last night. George told my cousin, "You had a good day with him yesterday." My cousin, on a Sunday, was attempting to get the will changed. I left my mother with her brother alone while my cousin and I went to the cafeteria. The doctors agreed that he was of sound mind to change the will. My cousin went through the phone book in an attempt to get a lawyer to come to the hospital on a Sunday. Sound impossible? He could not find even one to come. But nothing is impossible with God.

My uncle was making plans to go to Florida with my cousin. The next minute he would talk about cremation. He was vacillating between hope and reality. The doctors came in and bluntly told my uncle, "You are dying. We need to discuss how and who will make your final decisions." My cousin was told that his liver had failed, and it was just a matter of time before his kidneys failed as well.

George told us, "We'll do whatever it takes to fix this; just have Faith."

I said, "Just believe, you gotta believe."

He said, "Yes."

My cousin said, "It's in God's hands now. It's not about the money. We did all that we can do. I have to trust God will work it all out the way He wants it to. I'm not going to worry about it."

I said, "There's got to be someone, somewhere who can help us."

My cousin said, "I forgive him. I love him."

"Love covers a multitude of sins," and forgiveness opens a door (1 Peter 4:8 NASB). While he said that, unbeknownst to us, George said he got a hold of the lawyer. I told George, "You are the angel sent to us by God. Thank you for everything you've done."

While I was taking my mother to the bathroom, I called my sister, a legal secretary, and she said, "It's too late. You'll never get the will changed now." I was angry, but still, I prayed and hoped. When we got back from the bathroom, the lawyer was there! The lawyer was under the impression that the will had already been changed, but I told him it had not been changed. He called his daughter and realized the error and then had my uncle rewrite the will back into his son's name!

As soon as my cousin left it up to God and trusted Him, He performed the miracle. How Great is Our God!

My mother and I left the hospital for home because I now had to go back to work the next day. God used me as an instrument to bring about His will, and I was glad.

My cousin told his father, "Screw my business, I'm here, and I Love You, and I'll be here for you as long as it takes." I received a text from my cousin on Monday, saying that his dad passed away that morning at 10:26 a.m. and how he held his hand and told him he loved him and that he will be in heaven with his dog, Molly. I was in orientation class and had to leave the room to compose myself. I texted my cousin back and told him that God orchestrated this whole thing from the nurse finding you, to getting the will changed, to you reconciling with your father, and having him receive Jesus as his Lord and Savior before he died. Now, he can rest in peace.

The Holy Spirit provides us with gifts and fruits. As St. Paul tells the Galatians to live by the Spirit and not the desires of the flesh. Fruits of the Spirit are those supernatural works done joyfully and with peace of soul. They should be a virtuous act performed with pleasure. The fruits of the Spirit are "love, joy, peace, patience, kindness, goodness, faithfulness, gentleness, and self-control..." (Galatians 5:22–23 NASB). Those who belong to Christ Jesus do not follow the desires of the flesh but live in the Spirit:

The gifts of the Spirit are those gifts given by God for the good of all and given for some benefit. They are: wisdom, knowledge, faith, healing, mighty deeds, prophecy, discernment of spirits, varieties of tongues, interpretation of tongues (1 Corinthians 12:7–10). The Holy Spirit produces all of these, distributing them individually to each person as He wishes. I believe it is the Holy Spirit who inspired me to write this book.

It's not about religion. It's all about relationship. It's about your relationship with Jesus Christ and all else that comes with it.

*"Then John said in reply, "Master, we saw someone casting out demons in your name and we tried to prevent them because he does not follow in our company" So Jesus said," "Do not prevent him, for whoever is not against you is for you."*
(Luke 9:49–50 NABRE)

So, I believe that it doesn't matter if you're Baptist, Episcopalian, Catholic, Lutheran, or Born-Again. If you are Christian, a follower of Jesus Christ, and attend a Bible-based church, it shouldn't matter what faith you practice. If you believe that Jesus Christ is your Lord and Savior and repent of your sins, you are "saved". Because the only way to the Father is through the Son; Jesus is "...the Way, the Truth, and the Life" (John 14:6 NLT). That is how one gets to heaven.

With every superhero comes an adversary—a Villain. Satan, the devil, is God's adversary. He was once an angel, named Lucifer (Latin word for morning star) or Satan, who fell from God's grace. He wanted to become equal to God and have all His power. Talk about prideful ambition! He was cast out of heaven (Isaiah

14:12–15). He roams the earth, searching to steal souls from God to accompany him to Hell (1 Peter 5:8). He tempted Adam and Eve and had her eat the forbidden fruit, telling her she would not die but become like God Himself (Genesis 3:5). She believed it, and the first sin was committed. Then there was Job, who had it all! He had children, many cattle, oxen, sheep, and riches. He was a faithful man of God. God was so pleased with Job that He allowed Satan to take away all that he had except his life (Job 2:6). Job lost his family and all the riches he had (Job 1:14–19). Job endured much suffering, including horrific sores on his body (Job 2:9). Even his wife told him to curse God (Job 2:9). But he would not. Later, God restored everything to Job, giving him twice as much as what he had (Job 42:10).

God sent His only Son to us as payment for our sins. By shedding His blood on the cross, He became the sacrificial lamb (John 1:29). Satan had the audacity to even tempt Jesus (God Himself) in the desert (Matthew 4:3). But Jesus rebuked the devil by quoting Scripture each of the three times the devil tried to tempt Jesus (Luke 4:4, 8, 12). Jesus cast out a legion of demons (who recognized Him as Lord), out of the man from Garasene (Mark 5:7–13). He placed them into pigs, and they ran off the cliff into the sea and drowned (Luke 8:28, 33). God knows our weaknesses and that we would be subject to temptation by the devil. He knew we are only human and subject to failure and sin. He knew the devil would tempt us as he did Jesus in the desert.

When Jesus died, the veil was torn in half, and we can now talk to our God again (Matthew 27:51). This is why Jesus said, "I will ask the Father and he will give you another Advocate to be with you always, the Spirit of truth, which the world cannot accept because it neither sees nor knows it." (John 14:16 NABRE). Oh, for those who think Satan is a myth, just look around you; violence, prejudice, murders, the killing of the unborn, pornography, etc. The list goes on and on. St. Peter said, "Your opponent, the devil is prowling around like a lion for someone to devour" (1 Peter 5:8 ISV).

But Good always conquers Evil because prayer is our greatest weapon. When we pray, we acknowledge God as the supreme being able to hear and meet our needs. We pray for answers, for healing, for gratitude, for help in our day-to-day struggles. Pray to God the Father through Jesus Christ in the Holy Spirit. Pray without ceasing as St. Paul writes (1 Thessalonians 5:17).

My Heroine is Mary, the virgin child who said "yes" to the angel Gabriel when he announced to her that she was to become the mother of the Son of God (Luke 1:26, 27). She had no idea how that was to come about because she had never had relations with a man. But anything is possible. She said, "Behold, I am the handmaid of the Lord. May it be done to me according to your word" (Luke 1:38 NABRE). What faith! In her day, she could have been stoned to death for being pregnant and not married. And what about her fiancée Joseph? How he must have felt knowing he was not the father. The people in the town must have been mocking her and calling her a liar. An angel did come to Joseph to tell him that Mary was telling the truth (Matthew 1:20). But Mary had no idea what her life would be like. Mary was nine months pregnant when she rode a donkey all the way to Bethlehem, which was about a three-day journey, all because of a Roman census! (Luke 2:4–5). I wonder if Mary was rethinking this whole thing when they finally arrived, and there is no room at the inn. I don't know about you, but I would have liked a nice shower. Better yet, she is now in labor! So, she gives birth in a cave amongst the farm animals and wraps Him in swaddling clothes, and lays him in a manger (Luke 2:7). His name is Jesus.

But her troubles do not end there. Joseph is told in a dream that King Herod wants to kill Jesus, and they must flee now, just like our refugees of today (Matthew 2:13). They flee to Egypt and escape Herod's killing of all children two years old and under (Matthew 2:16). When King Herod dies, an angel of the Lord appeared to Joseph once more, telling him, "...Go to the land of Israel..." (Matthew 2:20 ESV). He went to the land of Israel but heard that Archelaus was ruling in place of his father Herod and was warned in a dream, so he went to the region of Galilee, to the town of Nazareth (Matthew 2:22–23). Here they can finally call home.

At some point, it is believed that Mary was a single mother because Joseph, who was thought to be much older than she, we assume dies. I can relate to Mary being a single mom for a period of time and all that comes with it. I can relate to how afraid she was for her son facing persecution. But I cannot and would never be able to understand how she witnessed her beloved son whipped with the flagrum of Roman soldiers, carry his cross, and watched as each nail pierced his hands and feet to hang on a cross (John 19:1, 17; Matthew 27:35). I cannot fathom how she endured the pain, agony, and immeasurable grief! I would have lost my mind! Her only son murdered! For the sake of others? It seems grossly unfair, cruel, and unimaginable. But her courage, faith, and trust in God did not falter. She is the mother of Jesus Christ, Son of God, and we are his brothers and sisters, which makes Mary our mother also. It is simple; A plus B equals C. Mary was not just a nice Jewish girl, she was filled with God. Mary is the only person on this earth that was filled with God three times. She was impregnated by the Holy Spirit, she carried Jesus in her womb for nine months, and she was filled with the Holy Spirit, once again at Pentecost in the upper room (Luke 1:35, 2:7; Acts 1:13–14). This alone brings her far above all the angels and saints.

If you were to ask your son to do something for you, wouldn't he do it? Eventually, yes. Didn't Jesus turn water into wine at the wedding of Cana just because his mother asked him to? (John 2:1–9). How much more do you think He would do if His mother asked Him to? Through her son Jesus Christ. She, in fact, has appeared to seventy thousand people at Fatima. Even nonbelievers and reporters report it was, in fact, a miracle. In the pouring rain, she had the sun dance in the sky and completely dry up all the water and the peoples' clothes who were drenched.[20] She has appeared many other times as well, all over the world to many other people.[21] She has performed many documented miracles as well. She appeared to St. Bernadette in Lourdes, France, curing the sick from the spring.[22] In Mexico, Our Lady of Guadalupe appeared to Juan Diego so that when he opened his cloak, her image was impressed in it as a miracle of authenticity of the apparitions.[23] She is the reason

20 "Miracle of the Sun, Fatima, Portugal, October 13, 1917." n.d. *Wikipedia, The Free Encyclopedia*. 2020. https://en.wikipedia.org/wiki/Miracle_of_the_Sun.
21 "Our Lady of Lourdes." 2020. *Wikipedia, The Free Encyclopedia*. 2020. https://en.wikipedia.org/wiki/Our_Lady_of_Lourdes.
22 Ibid.
23 "Our Lady of Guadalupe." 2020. *Wikipedia, The Free Encyclopedia*. 2020. https://en.wikipedia.org/wiki/Our_Lady_of_Guadalupe.

we pray the rosary. She is our best intercessor with her Son, Jesus. And yes, she has prayers answered also.

Mary's life was anything but ordinary or easy. But she endured and persevered everything that this life threw at her with humility and faith. She is a heroine in my book.

As I knelt down in prayer at the Shrine of Our Lady one day, I was staring at Jesus on the cross, when it hit me, Jesus was hanging there broken in both spirit and body. When He said, "My God, my God, why have you forsaken me?" (Matthew 27:46 ESV), with His death imminent and the wounds on his body from the lashing of the cat-of-nine tails (Matthew 27:26), the crown of thorns around his head, (John 19:2) and the nails in his hands and feet (John 20:20)... I thought, *How beautifully broken He was.* I believe that is why Jesus is close to the brokenhearted.

# CHAPTER 5

# Desert Storm

Desert: dry, desolate land, few forms of life; noun. Empty, uninhabited, deserted, abandon, forsaken; verb.[24]

Storm: violent disturbance of the atmosphere, upheaval. Tumultuous reaction, commotion, disturbance, furor, trouble, hue.[25]

Have you ever felt your life was "thrown a curve ball" as my father used to say? And a storm or a crisis has hit you? Have you ever felt alone, abandoned, afraid, lost, or broken, forgotten, unworthy, or unloved? Something hits you; an unwelcomed crisis or catastrophe hits you. If you have, you've been hit by a storm and have walked in the desert for a "season," a desert storm. I've walked in the desert after being hit by a storm more times than I would have liked in my life. But... God has always been there for me. For He said,

*Have I not commanded you? Be strong and of good courage; do not be afraid, nor be dismayed; for the Lord your God is with you wherever you go.*

(Joshua 1:9 NKJV)

---

24 "Desert." n.d. Merriam-Webster Online Dictionary. Merriam-Webster, Incorporated. Accessed October 20, 2020. https://www.merriam-webster.com/dictionary/desert.
25 "Storm." 2020. Merriam-Webster Online Dictionary. Merriam-Webster, Incorporated. 2020. https://www.merriam-webster.com/dictionary/storm.

*Never will I leave you; never will I forsake you.*

(Hebrews 13:5 NIV)

It has been said that it is written 365 times in the Bible to not fear, tremble, be afraid. Even Jesus said,

*In this world you will have tribulation; but be of good cheer, I have overcome the world.*

(John 16:33 NKJV)

Life isn't always smooth sailing. Even people in the Bible have walked in the desert. Faith is being able to walk through the storm to the other side.

Take Hagar, the servant of Abram's wife, Sarai. Sarai was beyond childbearing age, and since God promised Abram he was to be a father of nations, Sarai did not feel this was possible. Sarai did not walk by faith but by sight. She had Abram have intercourse with Hagar, and she bore him a son named Ismael (Genesis 16:15). The Lord changed Abram's name to Abraham and Sarai's name to Sarah (Genesis 17:5, 15). When Sarah, at age ninety, bore a son just as God had promised, they named him Isaac (Genesis 21:3). Sarah learned firsthand that nothing is impossible for God. Sarah grew jealous of the relationship between Abraham and Ismael and told Abraham that Hagar and her son had to leave (Genesis 21:10). Hagar was forced into the desert with her son, and when all her provisions were gone, she was preparing to die (Genesis 21:16). "God heard the lad crying; and the angel of God called to Hagar from heaven and said to her, "What is the matter with you, Hagar? Do not fear, for God has heard the voice of the lad where he is. Arise, lift up the lad, and hold him by the hand, for I will make a great nation of him." (Genesis 21:17, 18 NASB). God was with the boy as he grew up. He lived in the wilderness and became an expert bowman with his home in the wilderness of Paran.

His mother got a wife for him from the land of Egypt (Genesis 21:20, 21). Hagar was physically and spiritually in a desert storm. She must have felt abandoned, forgotten, and lost, but God provided for her and her son. When we do not see a way, God makes a way.

Poor Joseph was hit by a storm when he was sold for twenty pieces of silver as a slave by his own brothers! (Genesis 37:28). He was blindsided and walked into his desert. He was innocent of Potiphar's wife's accusations of sexual advances towards her. He was sent to prison for something he did not do (Genesis 39:19, 20). Talk about feeling forsaken by the Lord, and certainly, he had every right to. But Joseph kept his faith. The Lord was with him and brought him out of his desert with his gift of interpretation of dreams. Joseph interpreted Pharaoh's dream of famine and plenty, and he became second in charge under Pharaoh (Genesis 41:29–31, 41).

Joseph forgave his brothers when they came for food during the famine and showed them mercy by giving them food (Genesis 45:15). He was rewarded by being able to see his father and youngest brother again (Genesis 46:30). Thus, his dream of them bowing down to him was fulfilled.

Moses was raised in the palace of Pharaoh by Pharaoh's daughter when he was found in the Nile river (Exodus 2:5–6). Moses, who reacted to the beating of a fellow Israelite, killed that Egyptian guard (Exodus 2:12). Bam! The storm hit, and now he has to flee into the wilderness or desert (Exodus 2:15). Here, he has made a life for himself, was married, and had a family (Exodus 2:21–22). Now God speaks to him from a burning bush and wants him to free His people from Egypt (Exodus 3:4, 10). Moses must have had a million reasons NOT to go back to Egypt, and he probably felt unworthy because he had a speech impediment (Exodus 4:10). He surely couldn't speak to Pharaoh and attempt to persuade him to let His people go! I'm sure he had his doubts too because Pharaoh did not care about his God. He had his own gods. On top of that, he must have been a little afraid! But he obeyed the Lord, and with his brother Aaron's help and the Lord's plagues against Pharaoh, Moses did lead His people out of Egypt by the parting of the Red Sea (Exodus 14:21). But he wandered for forty years in the desert! (Joshua 5:6). He knew his

God was with him as God spoke to Moses many times during those forty years.

Even David, as a young shepherd boy with only his faith in God and his five stones and a slingshot, killed the biggest giant, Goliath, and saved his people (1 Samuel 17:40, 50). He was anointed to be king. His storm hits when King Saul became jealous of him with his victories in battle and tries to have him killed (1 Samuel 18:19). Now David has to hide in caves because he is being hunted by the kings' soldiers (1 Samuel 22:1). David finally proves to the king that he could have killed him, but he did not. (1 Samuel 24:11). So, even David, a man after God's heart, had to walk in his desert. He must have thought, *How can I be king while I'm living like a caveman?* He must have had his doubts and reservations thinking, *Am I really to be king?* Later, David does become a mighty God-fearing king of Jerusalem, reigning for forty years until his death, and his son Solomon is appointed king (2 Samuel 5:3, 5:4; 1 Kings 1:39).

Then there was Job, who had it all. A God-fearing man (Job 1:1). Satan tried to get Job to renounce God. Satan took away all his livestock, Job's children, and he had boils on his skin (Job 1:14–17, 19, 2:7). How he must have felt forgotten and unloved by God. But Job remained faithful to God. Even his wife told him to curse God (Job 2:9). Through his walk in the desert, rather than curse God, he cursed himself and wished he were never born (Job 3:11). God saw his perseverance and faithfulness, and God gave him back double of everything in which he had lost (Job 42:10). He was the richest man in the East.

Even Jesus, the Son of God, spent time in the actual desert, forty days and nights, alone praying (Matthew 4:1, 2). Even He was tempted by the devil himself (Matthew 4:3). He rebuked him, of course, by quoting scripture (Matthew 4:4). But I wonder if He felt afraid or had second thoughts about the whole crucifixion thing. But He knew who He was and who God is and of His purpose here on this earth. He chose it anyway because of Love. Love kept Him on the cross for us to be saved from sin. He could have twelve legions of angels take Him off the cross at any time He deemed so (Matthew 25:53). But Love for us kept Him on that cross, not nails because love is the greatest force of all. "...Faith, hope and love. But the greatest of these is love" (1 Corinthians 13:13 NIV). He surely put that to the test! So, He knows whatever the struggle you are going through: be it an addiction, abuse, divorce, mental illness, depression, loss of a family member, a financial struggle, illness, a faith issue, a period of being in "the desert". He is there for you; only a prayer away. Remember, it is only for a "season".

Saul, now St. Paul, was hit by his storm when he was knocked off his horse and blinded for three days

(Acts 9:9). He then literally saw the light! (Acts 9:3). He then, instead of hurting Christians, he became one. He sought out Ananias and was given his sight back (Acts 9:18). Once converted, he preached in foreign lands about Jesus performing many miracles. He was imprisoned for his beliefs, where he wrote much of the New Testament to the many churches, always encouraging and directing them in the way of the Lord.

I think the Holy Spirit helped him write it. St. Paul never even saw Jesus but heard about Him through St. Peter and others. I wonder if he ever felt deserted, unloved, afraid, or alone in his prison cell in Rome. Later, it is believed that he was beheaded. We take our beliefs for granted, but most of us are not being thrown in jail or beheaded for being a Christian. Through all of this, he never gave up his faith.

Although tested by trials and tribulations, may your faith be found to continue to praise and worship our Lord Jesus Christ even in the storm and through the desert. If you feel your prayers are not being heard, be assured that they are. Throw in a little praise. Sometimes a little praise and even some fasting are the extra efforts we need to make.

We all get hit by a storm of one kind or another in our life. We all go through a period of being in the desert, as I like to call it. But we walk through it with God's help. People in a crisis either turn to God or away from

Him and blame Him. I've learned that our desert or wilderness is a preparation from God, not a punishment. It is for the future planning. God is not putting you on the sidelines. "Process is the wilderness to fulfill His promise," as I heard one preacher state.

If Moses wasn't picked up by the Pharaoh's daughter and groomed and educated as an Egyptian, he would not have had the skill set to lead God's people out of Egypt to the promised land (Acts 7:22). In the interim, he spent forty years in the wilderness, making a life for himself there (Acts 7:30). The desert is preparation for something bigger and better usually. His ways are not our ways and beyond our understanding (Isaiah 55:8, 9). Sometimes I feel that it is a test to see how we will handle the small storms, so when the larger ones come in our life, we will be ready. Will we curse God or praise Him in the storm and remain faithful to Him? God loves us, and sometimes He gives us the desert storm to us as a time out to teach us something such as humility or perseverance, to believe in hope again, and to put our trust in Him. Leave all anxiety and fear and lay it down at the foot of the cross. The song *I Will Fear No More* by The Afters sings of this.[26] I have many times been in a desert storm, but I always knew that God was with me.

---

26 "Afters - I Will Fear No More Lyrics by Joshua Havens, Jason Ingram, Jordan Mohilowski, Matt Fuqua, and Dan Ostebo – 2018." n.d. Metrolyrics. 2020. https://www.metrolyrics.com/i-will-fear-no-more-lyrics-afters.html.

On August 9, 2017, I wrote:

*The Desert*
*That's when God speaks*
*the Loudest when you're alone...*
*In need...*
*Leaning on Him in quiet*
*Desperation...*
*Baring your Soul to Him*
*Hoping for*
*His protection...*
*His Love...*
*His presence...*
*To pour into*
*Your Life.*

I've felt alone most of my life. Alone as a teenager, the eldest of six siblings. I was the babysitter for them. My mom and dad were always consumed with the next child and the diapers and feedings, etc. I felt alone in four different high schools. I ran away alone. Alone when I was molested, alone when I lost my first love, and then my second, my husband. I've felt abandoned with my divorce, even though I had supportive friends and family. But they didn't know my pain and tears in the middle of the night with two boys, ages sixteen and twelve, to raise alone and make ends meet on my sal-

ary. I've felt unworthy, lost, broken, and unloved. But...
I never felt that God was NOT there, somewhere behind the scenes, with His Grace making the numbers
work, and all would be well. "...Beauty for Ashes..." (Isaiah 61:3 NKJV), as the Bible says. The beautiful song I
will, by Citizen Way tells us that "God will always carry
us through the darkness 'till we see the sun again (...)
when you can't lift that weight, believe me when I say,
I Will."[27] meaning He will do it for us. He will always
help us.

Somewhere between doing homecare nursing and
washing my mother's clothes from the nursing home, I
got bedbugs in my house. This was really a desert storm
for me. I abhor bugs. To top it off, I was allergic to the
bites. I didn't know what it was at first, but by the process of elimination, I figured it out. My nose, ears, and
eyes were itchy red and excoriated. The bites all over
my body and face, the itching was unbearable. At first,
the doctor thought I caught scabies from a patient and
gave me Kwell lotion to put all over your body for twelve
hours and then wash off. My son Ronnie had to do it
too, just in case. That did not work. A man with a spe-
cialized dog came who found the bedbugs by sniffing
them out. He came for $450 and made a positive as-

---

27 "Citizen Way - I Will Lyrics, Written by Ben Calhoun and Jeff
Pardo, Released 2016." n.d. Azlyrics.Com. 2020. https://www.azlyr-
ics.com/lyrics/citizenway/iwill.html.

sessment. Every night at 3 a.m. I would awake itching
(that is when they come out to feed). The whole idea
just made me sick. I couldn't sleep or eat. I lost twenty
pounds. I couldn't go out. I couldn't be with family or
friends in fear of infecting them. I had gotten fleas in
my house from a patients' home who had wild feral cats
in her house. That comparatively, was an easy fix. Bathe
the dogs, throw out the futon where they slept, and fog
the house and clean. But this was another whole matter, which I was not prepared for.

The exterminator cost was $1500 for the house to
be sprayed and another $500 for my car. I had to put
the dogs in my car and drive around with them for four
hours while they sprayed. It was the winter, and it was
too cold to leave them outside. After many doctor and
dermatology visits later: the throwing out of bedding
and clothes, I was washing clothes every day, shower-
ing three to five times a day, cleaning every day, in-
specting my clothes and sheets before putting them on,
I had learned that one bug could lay hundreds of eggs!
I had a dream where a voice said, "Throw out the bed
frame." I awoke, and my son Ronnie helped me after we
had already thrown out the head and footboards.

I had read to put boric acid around the bed, which I
put on the metal frame that I now had. The extermina-
tors came once a month for six months, but it took over
a year for me to be fully free of them. I bought store-

bought spray and sprayed that too. I can tell you I almost lost my mind. I felt like a leper with bites all over my face, arms, legs, and back, alienated from friends and family, unwelcomed anywhere and unloved.

I asked God, "Why?" I dug into the Scriptures more; I prayed more; I watched TBN and EWTN more than ever. My mantra became "Pray and Spray!" This went on for about one and a half years. I prayed and prayed for Gods' strength, courage, and mercy to get me through this. I knew, "This too shall pass," but when? Eventually, I threw out all my bedroom furniture. And for about six months had only the metal bedframe in my room and a plastic two drawers for my light, Bible, and writing materials. It looked so bare; it reminded me of a monks' room. I eventually bought new mattresses, box springs for myself and my boys. I thank God I had the money to pay for it all.

My son had just gotten a new puppy, and I was afraid the bugs would bite him and my other older dog, but the exterminator told me, "No, they don't bite animals." I read later that they do. I learned humility from all of this. Also, I learned that it's not important to have your nails, hair, makeup done. It doesn't matter. There are more important things like sleep and being able to have peace of mind.

I have to use special prescription creams now on my skin and hair, I have dry eye syndrome, and I have to take a sleeping pill to sleep. I also now have deep wrinkles and scars on my face. I felt like Job when my family didn't want me for Christmas (and rightly so). It just hurt me to the core, even now, I get teary-eyed just thinking about it. Because Christmas has always been my holiday and it's usually the most joyous time for me. I cried and cried. I said the devil will not win this war. I showered and went to Mass and sat in the last row (my go-to now), and went out to dinner with my best friend Amber, her family, and my two sons. And when each day would pass, and I would awaken with new bites on my body, I would say, "God, I can't do this anymore." Then I'd say, "No, SATAN, you will not win." I'd say to myself, "I can do all things through Christ who strengthens me" (Philippians 4:13 NKJV).

My sister Christine said her pastor said, "If the devil is not chasing you, you're not doing the Lord's work." I knew I was doing the Lords' work ministering to the sick, the homeless, the depressed, and the mentally ill. Music and songs were my inspiration. A song would come on always right on time when I needed it. Like one song said, "Let your tears fall like rain in a pool of grace."[28] I don't know why I'm going through what I am, but only God knows. I awoke one morning in March 2017 and heard the Holy Spirit say, "You are worthy of

---

28 "Matt Hammitt - Tears Lyrics, 2017." n.d. Azlyrics.Com. 2020. https://www.azlyrics.com/lyrics/matthammitt/tears.html.

this trial, consider yourself among the few that are wor-thy." A great joy entered my heart. May all the anguish and pain be for the glory of God. I always knew God was with me in the desert... and I've felt His presence even in times of abandonment.

On May 6, 2018, the Holy Spirit gave me these words as I wrote: "Even in the Desert."

*Even in the Desert*
*He is always with me*
*Even in the Desert*
*He always cares,*
*Even in the desert*
*My Heart always knows*
*That even in the desert*
*He is always there.*
*I've been in the desert*
*A time or two*
*And I know the feeling*
*That's it's not a comfortable one*
*But, still I know*
*That it's in the desert, I will grow,*
*For keeping the Faith*
*Is to walk in darkness*
*Knowing that on the other side*
*Is the Light...*
*You have to walk through the desert*

*Before you get to the oasis*
*The walk through the desert*
*Is a lonely but a necessary one...*
*Because your walk through the desert*
*Brings you ever so closer to our Lord*
*Jesus Christ.*
*The walk through the desert*
*Refines your humility, patience, perseverance, and Love*
*The walk through the desert*
*Is not how the world sees it*
*Entrusting and surrendering your*
*Life into His hands.*

I've learned that with God on your side, you always win. It takes perseverance and trust in your afflictions. I read Hebrews 10:36 (NABRE), "You need endurance to do the will of God to receive what he has promised." Also, in James 1:2–4 (NABRE), "Consider it all joy my brothers, when you encounter various trials; for you know that the testing of faith produces perseverance. And let perseverance be perfect, so that you may be perfect and complete lacking in nothing". Then I heard a pastor say, "What the devil tries to steal from you, the Lord will restore." I said to myself, "He tried to steal my mind more than once; maybe you, Lord want me to write about it for others." I also read, "Focus your attention on Jesus' wonderful love and let Him lift your

Heart to grateful worship in the midst of pain."[29] The more you draw closer to God, the more He draws closer to you. So, I worshipped through music and songs. Then Michael W. Smith's song came on the radio *Surrounded* and spoke to me. Words started to come out of my mouth, i.e., "This is how I fight my battles,"[30] and I'd say "On my knees," he'd continue to sing it again, and I'd say, "Praising," and again, "Believing," "Praying," "Surrendering," "Forgiving," etc. Then when he got to "When it feels like I'm surrounded, I'm surrounded by You," I'd say, "Beauty, grace, mercy, truth, or love after each verse. I believe it was the Holy Spirit speaking, even though I haven't told Michael yet.

It reminded me of *Footsteps in the Sand* poem where the man has a dream of his life. He sees two sets of footprints in the sand, and then when life was the hardest and the most painful, he saw only one set of footprints.[31] He asked, Lord, I thought you said you would never leave me. How come there was only one set of footprints in the sand when life was the toughest?[32] The

---

29 "Quote by Joe Stowell, ODB: The Great Creator-Healer." 2014. Why Am I [YMI]: Our Daily Bread Ministries. 2014. https://ymi. today/2014/02/odb-the-great-creator-healer/.

30 "Surrounded (Fight My Battles) Lyrics by Michael W. Smith, Released 2018." n.d. AZLyrics.Com. 2020. https://www.azlyrics.com/ lyrics/upperroom/surroundedfightmybattles757618.html.

31 "Footprints in the Sand (Poem)." 2020. *Wikipedia, The Free Encyclopedia*. 2020. https://en.wikipedia.org/wiki/ Talk%3AFootprints_(poem).

32 Ibid.

Lord answered him by saying, "Those my son, are the times I carried you."[33] So... I think He has carried me this far and through my desert to the other side for a definite reason.

I remember reading *The Shack* by William Paul Young in 2007. I gave the book to all my closest friends to read because I thought it was a great book. Now, ten years later, it is a movie! They were even giving out copies of the book at my brother's Catholic church. I caught the TBN special about it with William Paul Young, the author. The author only intended it for his family. He went on to say how the shack represents our heart, our soul that is broken. Everyone matters to God. When I went to see the movie with a friend, the pivotal moment for me was when Papa said to Mack, "I've never left you, and I love you so much." Tears just ran down my face. I cried silently, knowing God loves even me, although I couldn't feel it. I was so busy trying to love others in my care; I forgot that I too was loved. "God uses adversity to purify our faith," I heard Charles Stanley on TBN say, and "Affliction purifies your faith." "Your faith will be purified and strengthened through afflictions," he added.

The Lord has carried me through more times than I could not work and provided for me anyway. I've learned to lean on Him more and more and trust Him

---

33 Ibid.

more. I've decided to praise and worship and be thankful. "I can do all things in Christ who strengthens me" became my mantra while undergoing total hip replacement surgery (Philippians 4:13 NKJV). In the dark hours, watching the clock tick by each and every hour, lying there awake in pain, listening to the devil whisper to me of how I had a blood clot in my lungs and how I wouldn't make it through the night and how very anxious I became, I knew that He had the final say and I just prayed. Because crying endures but for a night, but joy comes in the morning (Psalm 30:5). It wasn't exactly joy, but it was better than night. I couldn't take pain medications, so I was only given Tylenol IV. I don't know how, but I endured it and prayed through it. With His Grace, I suppose. I heard someone say, "With Grace comes Wisdom." After the second surgery, which went a whole lot better than the first, I had a window to look out of. As I looked out my hospital window, I wrote on May 25, 2019:

*Thank you Jesus,*
*For a beautiful Sunrise,*
*I witnessed this morning.*
*Rays of Sun bringing Light and*
*Warmth to the Earth.*
*Brightening up the dark.*
*The World shines with a*

*Heavenly glow as every*
*Tree and flower yearn*
*For His Beauty.*

My best friend Tee had gotten colon cancer, stage 4. She underwent surgery and then chemo and radiation. I didn't have that, so I thanked God, it was just "bugs" and not cancer. On my worst day, I wasn't vomiting and battling nausea, pain, and death.

I remember one of my patients' who had just gotten an apartment but did not have any furniture. She was upset about it. I told her to just be thankful for what she does have. She has a roof over her head and food. "A grateful heart is a happy heart," I told her. She said, "Yes, thank you; I will remember that."

I am thankful for all the things, Lord, you have given me, and I will list them. My children, my family, my friends, my home, my job, my ability to provide for my kids, and to go on vacations together as a family. These, I feel, are the moments to treasure. It's being able to sing praise and be thankful even during the storms, whatever your storm is: some sort of addiction, abuse, pain, loneliness, mental illness, homelessness, medical problem, or financial burdens... Remember, it's only for a "season".

I had a patient with Congestive Heart Failure (CHF). His heart had failed to pump blood, and fluid accumulated in his chest. I drove up, and I saw a man in the snow taking little Christmas trees out of the back of his truck. I said to myself, "I really hope that isn't my patient." Sure enough, he was, and as he saw me, he ran into the house. He had his own business as a dog groomer with his own trailer, which he worked out of. He would go to his customer's houses and groom their dogs in his trailer, especially set up for that purpose. Now, he could not do that strenuous activity any longer. His storm hit now because he and his wife are losing their home, and without his income, they cannot pay the mortgage. His wife works part-time only. I needed to tell him he should not be lifting those trees in this cold weather out of his truck in this cold weather. He told me how he got the twenty trees for $20 and what a good buy he got.

So, the socioeconomic factors were a big blow to this family, and he was not yet processing the seriousness of his health issue. It turns out during my talks with him that he was in a men's Bible group. We had a common ground (as I was in a women's Bible group) to work with. He had his faith, and I reminded him that God cares for the birds of the sky; they do not worry about what they will eat; how much more does our Father care for you? (Matthew 6:26). I gave him a list of food pantries. He was computer savvy, and he found an organization that when you pay a certain amount of money, you get bags of groceries.

They had planned to move upstate and rent (cheaper to live), and stay with his wife's brother until he could get Social Security disability. He would have to sell his dog trailer or find someone to carry on the business. I reminded him of Romans 8:28 and how God works all things for our good for those who love him. When I left his house, I told him to read Romans 5:1–5 and told him it had helped me. He texted me the next day the same passage with the picture of the Twin Towers on fire which read,

*Therefore, since we have been justified through faith, we have peace with God through our Lord Jesus Christ, through whom we have gained access by faith into this grace in which we now stand. And we boast in the hope of the glory of God. Not only so, but we also glory in our sufferings, because we know that suffering produces perseverance; perseverance, character; and character, hope. And hope does not put us to shame, because God's love has been poured out into our hearts through the Holy Spirit, who has been given to us.*

(Romans 5:1–5 NKJV)

He said it was in his Bible group and sent it to his phone, and he sent it to me, stating, "It cannot be just a coincident." He wound up seeing a counselor for outpatient therapy. He was hit by a storm (his heart condition) and walked through his desert, and with God, he came out on the other side.

Another family was in crisis, and I was called to the ER by the charge nurse to come and minister to a 30 something-year-old male New York Police Department (NYPD) officer (post 9/11), who was found by his pregnant wife hanging in their basement. He now did not have any brain waves. His father, a New York fire department (NYFD) officer, who was also working post 9/11, blamed himself for not "seeing the signs". The father was so distraught all he could think about was going home to get his gun in order to take his own life, so he could be with his son. I convinced the wife to triage him because now he was suicidal, and I alerted security not to let him leave the hospital. The head psychiatrist and I spoke to him. We told him that it is not his fault, and now his son would not want him to do this. He was a firefighter and had saved countless lives to take his own would be meaningless. He should be thinking of his wife and handicapped daughter.

He came from a large Italian family, and all the uncles and aunts and cousins came to see their loved one, so we moved the son to a floor. He was on a vent supplying oxygen to his body, although his brain was already dead. This gave the family time to process what was to happen and a chance for relatives to say goodbye. The next morning the head pastor of the hospital called me to join him because the family was now ready to disconnect the tubing and "let him go". I bravely held their hands as the pastor prayed, and the other nurse turned off the machine. With tears in everyone's eyes, including mine, he stopped breathing. It was the hardest thing for me to do in my career—Partly because my brother was approximately the same age, an NYPD officer who also was in 9/11 sifting for remains. I called my brother and told him, "I loved him," and if he ever needed to talk about being in the aftermath of the World Trade Center that I was here for him. That family was hit by a huge storm and needed help in their desert walk.

As I listened to pastor Jentezen Franklin on TBN talk about his book *Love Like You've Never Been Hurt,* he stated that their family was hit by a storm (crisis) when their daughter left home.[34] He tells us that they were a mess, not knowing whether she was dead or alive.[35] He reports that his wife was in a fetal position on the couch for days.[36] He surprisingly got a phone call from his daughter, one day declaring that she was married.[37] He admits he was so hurt, but at least she was alive.

---

34 Franklin, Jentezen. 2018. *Love Like You've Never Been Hurt: Hope, Healing, and the Power of an Open Heart.* Bloomington, Minnesota: Chosen Books, a Division of Baker Publishing Group.
35 Ibid.
36 Ibid.
37 Ibid.

He explained that he now knows when someone asks him, "Please pray for my child," what that feels like.[38] He believes as do I, that we do NOT turn our backs on them, but that we LOVE them.[39] I believe that love is the answer.

I remember a time I felt far away from the Lord. I wasn't doing anything differently. It was that I was waiting for Him to tell me when and if I should quit my job. I went to see a priest about it, and he heard my confession. I told him that I felt I wasn't doing enough for the Lord and that He wasn't hearing me. He said, "It's ok, even Mother Teresa had feelings of being separated from the Lord, an emptiness, a dry period like a desert." (Unfortunately, it didn't make me feel any better). But the more I read Scripture, the more it pertained to me! The more the Lord was confirming things for me. For example, I obtained a four-wheel drive vehicle (lease) for my job, so I could drive in the snow because there are no "snow days" for nurses. Then I got something in the mail from a church that said something like, "God supplies all of our needs," which was so appropriate and right on time. This confirmed for me that it wasn't time to quit my job doing home care just yet.

My best friend's, Tee, colon cancer, had eventually spread to her lungs and bones. While we were en-route

---

38  Ibid.
39  Ibid.

to the oncologist's office one day, she would tell me that God doesn't hear her prayers anymore. I quickly and defiantly said, "Oh YES, He does. He just may not be giving us the answer we want, but He hears us." I also told her, "You know, you and I have been divorced, alone, single moms, making our own way, and being in charge of our lives at all times. I've learned that while being in the desert, I need to surrender and say, "God, I can't do this alone anymore; I'm laying this down at the foot of the cross for you to help me with your grace and mercy."

As I'm writing this, a song came on by Audrey Assad, *Drawn to You*. She sings, "After everything I've had, After everything I've lost, Lord, I know this much is true, I'm still drawn to you."[40] How powerful. It confirms what I am writing for—I'm writing for you. I'm writing for just one person to believe my truths, my encounters, my God, and to just... believe.

I was writing how we need more bolder evangelizers in America to preach the Word, more radically than ever before, like Paul to proclaim the gospel. Bishop Robert Baron agrees and has sermons on YouTube.[41]

---

40 Drawn To You by Audrey Assad, 2018." n.d. AZLyrics.com. 2020. https://www.azlyrics.com/lyrics/audreyassad/drawntoyou. html.

41 "Bishop Robert Barron - Word on Fire." n.d. YouTube. 2020. https://www.youtube.com/channel/UCcMjLgeWNwqL2LBGS-iPb1A.

Be the light in the darkness. This is the reason for my book—To evangelize by telling my story, my patients, my family, my friends, and acquaintances' experiences and encounters with our God.

CHAPTER 6

# He Speaks

The Lord still speaks. He speaks to us in many ways. We just have to stop and listen. We need to be aware of how, when, and where God speaks to us today. As Robert Morris has said in his book, *Frequency*, "Are you tuned in to the right frequency?"[42] We have to "tune in to His channel, His website, His satellite, His small voice." He speaks to us through His Word, the Bible,

---

42 Morris, Robert. 2016. Frequency. Thomas Nelson; First Edition first Printing (April 26, 2016). https://gatewaypeople.com/series/frequency-2016.

whispers or promptings through the Holy Spirit, other people, dreams, angels, answered prayers, and pain.

God spoke directly to Adam and Eve, Moses, Noah, David, to Jesus, and Peter, James, and John at the transfiguration (Genesis 2:16, 3:4, 6:13; 1 Samuel 23:2; Matthew 3:17; Luke 9:35). God also speaks indirectly through His prophets, Joshua, Elijah, Isaiah, and Jeremiah (Joshua 1:1; 1 Kings 17:2; Isaiah 6:8; Jeremiah 1:7).

The Bible, the Word, "And the Word was made flesh," referring to Jesus as written in John's gospel (John 1:14 ESV). The Bible is God-breathed, which means it was the Holy Spirit who instructed those in the writing of it.

Have you ever opened a random page of the Bible, and it answered your problem? God is like that. He shows up and does miraculous and mysterious things. I know I have done it a couple of times, and I found the answer to the question I had. Do I suggest you do it all the time? No. There have been other times where I'd have to read quite some time to get my answer. But all the answers are in "The Book".

I put the TV on, and there was a preacher who said to the audience, "You, go and be the Esther's in this world. For such a time as this, you have been chosen to save His people" (Esther 7:3–4), and I took it as I should write this book. If it only touches one person, it would have been worth it.

Sometimes the Holy Spirit whispers to you (from inside your heart) and you, have just to listen to hear it. What I mean by that is you have to be attuned to His promptings or whispers, and you must believe that it is possible. The Holy Spirit was given to us to help us, guide us, inspire us, direct us, and give us gifts to use for His glory. He can speak to us and tell us things like, "Get my sister a phone" or "Take your mother to see her dying brother." You always have the choice of obeying or not. The Holy Spirit can inspire you to write, as well.

How about St. Joan of Arc, who heard God's voice and led armies into battle? I say, "You go, girl!" She was a peasant girl born in the east of France. Joan had said that she had visions from God to take back her home at eighteen years of age; she led the French army into many quick victories, which made her famous.[43] She was later turned over to the English, who deemed her a heretic, and burned her at the stake.[44] She was only nineteen years old.[45]

The Lord can choose pastors, priests, ministers, authors, songwriters, signs, and your everyday Christian friends to speak to us and others also.

Look at Billy Graham, who went to over 185 countries and territories worldwide and preached to 210 million

43 "Joan of Arc - Wikipedia." 2020. *Wikipedia, The Free Encyclopedia*. 2020. https://en.wikipedia.org/wiki/Joan_of_Arc.
44 Ibid.
45 Ibid.

people. It is estimated that 3.2 million people gave their lives to Christ at his crusades.[46]

There's also Pope Francis, who is a very different pope than prior popes and advocates for the poor and doesn't even live in the Papal apartments.[47] He lives with the Daughters (sisters) of Charity at Saint Martha's house on the grounds of the Vatican. He wanted a more modest place to live and to be closer to the people.[48] One might say he lives outside the box. He is the first Jesuit pope from St. Ignatius of Loyola's founder of the Society of Jesus. They believe in being like Jesus, thus the name, Jesuits, in serving with love, with vows of charity. Their motto in Latin, "Ad maiorem Dei gloriam" (AMDG). It means "For the greater glory of God," and that is why they do everything.

- Author Joseph F. Girzone in his book Joshua, visits each denomination of churches, including the synagogue.[49] He found real religion is in people's hearts and not in man-made laws that divide each of the churches from one another.[50] This is what Jesus was saying about the pharisees

46 "Billy Graham." 2020. *Wikipedia, The Free Encyclopedia.* 2020. https://en.wikipedia.org/wiki/Billy_Graham.
47 "Pope Francis." 2020. *Wikipedia, The Free Encyclopedia.* 2020. https://en.wikipedia.org/wiki/Pope_Francis.
48 "Pope Francis." 2020.
49 "Joseph F. Girzone." 2020. *Wikipedia, The Free Encyclopedia.* 2020. https://en.wikipedia.org/wiki/Joseph_F._Girzone.
50 Ibid.

and the sadducees. They cared more about their laws than living out the "Love for one another" that Jesus taught. Jesus wanted His church unified, not divided. Joshua states, "I feel drawn to all those people who are trying to bring love and unity back into the human family, wherever I find them."[51]

• The author Henri Nouwen once said, "One of the main tasks of theology is to find words that do not divide but unite, that do not create conflict but unity, that do not hurt but heal."[52]

• Nick Vujicic, author and inspirational speaker, was born without arms or legs.[53] Did God forget to put arms and legs on Nick in utero? I think not. Nothing God does is an accident. He did it on purpose. Nick found strength, courage, and resolve and a purpose for living. It is to help others. He is a Christian and a believer. And in the process, he found love, got married, and has two children! If you are one of those who are missing a limb, know that life is still beautiful and worth living.

---

51 Ibid.

52 "Henri Nouwen." 2020. *Wikipedia, The Free Encyclopedia.* 2020. https://en.wikipedia.org/wiki/Henri_Nouwen.

53 "Nick Vujicic." 2020. *Wikipedia, The Free Encyclopedia.* 2020. https://en.wikipedia.org/wiki/Nick_Vujicic.

- C.S. Lewis' book, *The Lion, the Witch and the Wardrobe*, from *The Chronicles of Narnia*, when you watch the film adaptation and just knowing that Aslan, the lion represents Jesus with all the good and that the witch represents the evil in the world, Satan...[54] It puts the whole movie into a very different perspective other than just a child's fantasy.

God also speaks through pastors and ministers. I remember I was praying about Jonathan going to Chicago to St. Ignatius of Loyola College. The sermon that week in which the pastor gave was about a man in Chicago. That was my sign that he would be alright going to Chicago alone.

I remember the time I was working two jobs. My nursing job at night and I was working as an N.Y. State daycare provider during the day. All of a sudden, I said to my husband, "My elbows hurt, isn't that strange?" Then it progressed to my knees and then to my hands, so much that I had great difficulty walking and changing a baby's diaper. I went to my chiropractor, who thought it was fibromyalgia. At the time, fibromyalgia was considered a figment of one's imagination, so to

---

54 Alexandra, Tanner. 2018. "The Lion, the Witch and the Wardrobe Study Guide , Literature Guide." LitCharts LLC. 2020. https://www.litcharts.com/lit/the-lion-the-witch-and-the-wardrobe.

speak. I did not accept that diagnosis, especially when one doctor recommended a psychiatrist. When it got to be too painful, and I was having trouble walking, "I said please, Lord, don't let me be in a wheelchair, my sons need their mother but... Your will be done, and I'll gladly take this on me rather than it happen to one of them." But then my chiropractor steered me towards a rheumatologist who then diagnosed me with rheumatoid arthritis. This was a sign to me that I needed to quit the daycare job and just do my nursing job.

Sometimes a song will come on that is right on time and is either an inspiration or a confirmation for me. Like when I was in the hospital room at night all alone. Tori Kelly's song Never Alone, came on and was a great comfort and reminder for me.

Sometimes, it's the people God puts in your path. He puts them there for a reason. We may not realize it at the time, but He knows the who and why He puts in our path. Sometimes they tell us things, sometimes we learn from them, sometimes we study with them, sometimes we pray with and for them. Everyone in your life is there for a reason, if only for a season.

My friend will send me a scripture verse of the day, and it's not just a coincidence that I just read it somewhere else, or I just wrote about it. Or sometimes, in my Bible group, the study will be something I had just read or wrote about or saw on TV or heard in Sunday's sermon.

I remember praying about our family trip to Australia. The church I was visiting was giving out Matthew Kelly's book, Rediscover Jesus. I was reading the book, when halfway through, I learned he was from Australia, owned a company in Chicago, and now lived in America with his family.[55] That was my sign that the trip would be within God's will. It was a God inspiring trip too!

Sometimes He speaks through signs—The parting of the Red Sea for the Israelites, proving that Moses was chosen by Him to lead them out of Egypt. The floods, tsunamis, volcanoes erupting, earthquakes are all signs of the end times. Like when I asked my friend Loretta to go with me to Israel because we'd been on the Africa adventure together, and I felt God wanted me to ask her. Every year Father R. led a group of men and women to Israel. I did not know any of them in the group. I felt compelled to visit the Holy Land when I found this out. I said to myself, *God, if you really want me to go and Loretta says yes, I will know it is from you.* When Loretta said, "Yes," it was confirmation that the trip was in the will of God.

When I first applied to another hospital for a per diem job, after retiring from one hospital, I went

---

55 Kelly, Matthew. 2015. *Rediscover Jesus: An Invitation.* Blue Sparrow, Beacon Publishing.

through the process of interviewing, and the nurse manager said, "Great, you can start on March 3." Later that week, I received a call from HR, stating, "I'm sorry, but we no longer have an opening for you." I said to myself, "That's strange, but OK, God; You know what you're doing." I'll admit I was upset for a little while. But I know that when God closes a door, He always opens a window.

So, I put in for traveling home care nurse. I thought maybe something different because I like to drive. Wouldn't you know it, I got the job and started the same day I was supposed to start the other job that I was turned down for.

Another sign, when I was writing my fourth chapter, I heard Matt and Laurie Crouch on TBN say something to the effect, "By telling your story, you are evangelizing."[56] When I was in the sixth chapter of the book and a priests' sermon at my church on Sunday was, "Get Out of Your Box and Serve the Lord." All these "signs" encouraged me every step of the way. All these are signs that told me God wants me to write this book to be published to serve as a testimony. I'm not one to get in front of a large crowd to speak (although I have done it on occasion under much duress). I'm more of

---

56 "Matthew and Laurie Crouch." 2020. *Wikipedia, The Free Encyclopedia.* 2020. https://en.wikipedia.org/wiki/Special:Search?search=%09Matthew+and+Laurie+Crouch&go=Go&ns0=1.

a one on one kind of person, and this book is my way of reaching the many; still on my personal one on one level. Just last week, I heard Pastor Robert Morrison on TBN say, "Learn to tell your story. When you share your story, people get saved."[57] That's what I'm trying to do.

God has always spoken to us through dreams and visions from Genesis to Revelation. The good news is that He still speaks to us today through our dreams. Some dreams are prophetic. Some dreams are a warning.

I've listened to Rabbi Schneider and his wife, who say that you should keep a journal next to your bed and write your dreams down as soon as you awake so as not to forget them.[58] You may not figure out the dream for years to come, but you'll have a record of it with the date on it. I think at some point, everyone in their lifetime has a dream. Most of the time, we forget it.

Even when I was a little girl, I'd say to my mother, "Haven't we done this already, or haven't we been here before?" She'd say, "No." It felt like I'd already seen this somewhere before, or been here before, whether in a dream or what's called *déjà vu*. I once dreamt that my husband had left me, and I awoke and reached over

---

57  "Robert Morris, Gateway Church (Texas)." 2020. *Wikipedia, The Free Encyclopedia*. March 9, 2020. http://gatewaypeople.com/profiles/robert-morris.
58  "Rabbi Schneider, Shaliach – A Jewish Messenger Of Jesus." 2020. Discovering the Jewish Jesus. 2020. https://discoveringthejewishjesus.com/about-2/rabbi-schneider/.

and felt him and said, "Oh, thank God." Years later, it came true. He was cheating on me and left to be with the other woman. That's a prophetic dream, or was it a warning dream?

When Joseph was young, he had a dream that his parents and siblings would bow down to him (Genesis 37:10). Many years later, he interpreted Pharaoh's dream of famine and plenty in the land. He was second in command under Pharaoh and was put in charge of the food. When his brothers came, they bowed down to him, asking for food. Thus, the fulfillment of Joseph's prophetic dream (Genesis 42:6).

Daniel interpreted King Nebuchadnezzar's dream of him losing his fortune and grazing on grass like an animal for seven years (Daniel 4:30–31). This, too, came to pass, another prophetic dream.

Joseph was told in a dream to leave Bethlehem. To take Mary and the baby to Egypt because King Herod was trying to kill Jesus (Matthew 2:13).

The Magi too, were warned in a dream to take another route home as not to pass by King Herod (Matthew 2:12).

Pilates' wife said she too had a dream that he should not have anything to do with the death of an innocent man, Jesus (Matthew 27:19). So, Pilate washed his hands and declared Jesus innocent, and His death fell on the people (Matthew 27:24).

I remember my son Ronnie and I were in Ireland when a cashier said to us, "Did you hear? Your Robin Williams killed himself?"[59]

I said, "What? You must be mistaken."

She said, "No, it's right here in the newspaper."

I found this too hard to believe. Not my Robin Williams. *The Mork from Ork.* The man who brought us the doctor with the red nose and who hired homeless people for extras in his movie, *The Fisher King.* The man who led Comic Relief for the poor and homeless. I had read somewhere that Robin Williams had bipolar disorder. The man whose highs were so high and his lows were even lower. Robin was the only man who could go toe to toe with Jonathan Winters off-script, and with his quick wit could make people fall off their chairs laughing so hard.[60]

In a world so broken, the man was a humanitarian bringing his gift to many. They say that laughter is the best medicine, and sometimes it is. I truly believe in my heart that this man who knew he had an incurable dis-

59 Robin Williams—Robin McLaurin Williams (July 21,1951–Aug.11, 2014 was an American actor and comedian. He began performing standup comedy during mid 1970's as an alien Mork from the sitcom Mork and Mindy (1978–1982). His cause of death: suicide by hanging. (www.wikipedia).

60 Jonathan Winters-Jonathan Harshman Winters III-American comedian, actor, author , television host and artist. He recorded many classic comedy albums for the Verve Record labels. (www.wikipedia)

LIVING OUTSIDE THE BOX

ease called Lewey Body dementia would not go to hell. I believe our God is more merciful than that. I prayed for him. A while later, I had a dream that Robin Williams and I were flying (which is not uncommon for me in my dreams), holding children in our arms and carrying them up to heaven. This was my sign that my Robin Williams was not in hell, and my prayer was answered, or so I hoped.

Another time, when I felt like Job, when I had bedbugs, I dreamt that I was on the beach on a blanket with an old-fashioned TV adjusting the antennae. In the water, I saw a Lion and the Lamb (Jesus) on it with birds, a deer, a tiger, and animals that normally wouldn't be together, floating together on a raft in the ocean. One by one, each of us swam up to the raft. When it was my turn, I said, "No. I'll just stay here," as I fiddled with the antennae ears and hand flipping the channels. I did not know what it meant at the time. I later surmised that I did not feel worthy to meet with our Lord because I felt "unclean" and "unworthy".

While in Africa, I felt I was in a frenzy. It was go, go, go, do, do, do, give, give, give, and then sleep and do it all over again. I felt the pace was a little too fast for me personally. I needed to slow down a bit to process where we were going and what we were giving to who. I had made this known. Well, that night, I dreamt I saw Jesus in a white robe sitting on a bench smiling at me.

133

I knew it was Him. I said, "I'm sorry, Lord, but I cannot stop and talk to You. I have to get this candy to the children!" Jesus just sat and smiled. Then I awoke, and I was so mad at myself for not stopping and spending time with Him, but He understood my mission and appeared to be pleased. I had stepped out of the boat, so to speak. I went with this mission group, but I did not know a soul before I went. I had some reservations, to begin with. But when we take that step of faith, God always takes the leap for us. So even in Africa, I knew God was with me.

My friend Renuka, was brought up in a Hindu household growing up in an Indian culture and lived in Trinidad. She remembers she had a 103 fever for five days, and during those days, she was unconscious. She dreamt she was sitting on Jesus' lap and told Him, "I'm hungry." Her fever cleared, and she awoke. She came to the U.S., and she got involved in a Christian church. I believe God showed her Jesus, and she was "hungry" for His word. She is now a deaconess and biblical counselor in her church.

And sometimes He sends an angel. Are angels real? Yes. Angels are mentioned in the Bible over 300 times! Angels are celestial beings sent to guide, protect, and direct us. I believe everyone has their very own guardian angel who watches over us individually. Some warn us, some guide us, and some just send us messages.

Satan or Lucifer, the Devil, was himself a fallen angel. He was an Archangel, which means he was "up there". His name originally meant morning star before he crashed and burned (Isaiah 14:12–14). He had so much power that he thought he could be God. But God abhors pride. God cast him and one-third of the angels who followed him out of heaven to earth. At the end of time, Satan will be cast into Hell with all who follow him. He, therefore, prowls around like a lion attempts to "steal souls" to accompany him in Hell (1 Peter 5:8).

Sound like a ghost story? Unfortunately, it is true. He is alive and well and if you don't believe in him, just look around. The random shootings of innocent people and children, the terrorist attacks, mothers killing their own babies by abortion, the slave trafficking of women and children, the easy access to pornography, drugs, alcohol, sex, the unbelief. It's all quite unbelievable, isn't it? But where do you think Evil comes from? It's in the center of the word DEVIL. Even Jesus believed in the devil and had not one but three encounters with him in the desert. Thankfully, we have St. Michael the Archangel to defend us in the battle against the devil (Revelation 12:7).

The Lords' messenger (angel) called out from heaven to Abraham, "Do not lay a hand on the boy..." when Abraham was going to sacrifice his only son to God (Genesis 22:12).

Angels appeared to Lot before the destruction of Sodom and Gomorrah (Genesis 19:12–13).

When Daniel was in the lion's den, "My God sent his angel and he shut the mouths of the lions" (Daniel 6:22 NIV).

In Jacob's dream, he saw Angels going up and down the ladder to heaven (Genesis 28:12).

An angel of the Lord appeared to Mary and said, "Behold you will conceive in your womb and bear a son and you shall call his name Jesus. He will be great and will be called the Son of the Most High" (Luke 1:31–32 ESV).

The angels appeared to the shepherds in the fields and told them to go to the stable under the Bethlehem star, and they would find a baby laid in a manger (Luke 2:10–12).

Jesus had angels ministering to Him in the desert where Satan was tempting Him (Matthew 4:11).

Two angels were at the empty tomb where Jesus was when Mary Magdalene arrived (John 20:12). They told her, "He is not here; he has been raised "(Luke 24:6 GNT).

Angels came to the prison where Peter was chained hand and foot and loosed his chains and walked him right past the guards and out the front door! (Acts 12:7–11).

Now you say, *Well, that was then in biblical times, not so in today's world*. Oh, ye of little faith. Angels are all around us. You are just unaware of their presence. They say that we've entertained angels but were probably unaware (Hebrews 13:2).

I'll tell you what happened to my children when they were in that horrific car accident where they and my ex-husband's truck was literally wrapped around a telephone pole. The medic said, "It's the worst I've ever seen. It's a miracle anyone survived." But after my son was cut out of the back of the truck and helicoptered to the hospital, he sustained only a head wound. He was discharged with staples in his head. My ex and my youngest son were sent via ambulance to another hospital. No broken bones on anyone. Thank God. My ex-husband may have been unconscious some of the time because he sustained a traumatic head injury. Later that night, I spoke to my kids individually as I tucked them into bed. They each separately told me that an old lady came to the window and said, "Don't worry, everything will be ok." When I questioned my husband, he said, "I didn't see anyone." I believe that she was an angel sent to calm my frightened children until the medics arrived. I believe God knew I could never recover from losing my husband and two children in a one-car accident, so He sent an angel.

I also believe that this man whom I will call him "Charlie," the guy at Dunkin' Donuts, whom I'd see every so often before work, would stand outside in the cold sometimes shivering despite the tattered, worn, and many layers of clothing he wore. One day, I asked him, "Would you like a cup of coffee to warm you?" He said, "Yes, I would!" I would buy him a cup of coffee and a donut every time I would see him thereafter. He said, "God bless you. Thank you so much." He had only a flip phone and said, "I'm waiting for my boss to call me in for work as a handyman." It was cold outside, and though he was dressed warmly, he said, "They won't let me go in and warm up." I hoped the coffee would warm him up some and suggested he warm up in a church. One day, as I handed him his coffee and donut, he was speaking on the phone and said, "This lady always buys me a cup of coffee and a donut when she sees me!" I don't know who he was talking to; was he possibly talking to God? Sometimes we entertain angels and are unaware.

About one year ago, approximately two weeks before Christmas, I had to go to Home Depot. I needed to get Christmas lights for the outside. This year because I was hosting Christmas Day at my house, I was short on cash and used my Home Depot charge card. I wasn't working anymore, so I had not been to Dunkin' Donuts in a while, and I forgot about "Charlie". Then there he was. He was in front of Home Depot, begging for money for food. I said, "I'm sorry, but I don't have any money, I'm using a charge card." I did my shopping, got my lights, and as I was paying for him, I said, "God, are you testing me to see if I will go to the bank and get money from the ATM and give it to him being that it's so close to Christmas and all?" I said, "Ok, Your will be done, not mine." So I went to the ATM got him some money and drove back to Home Depot, and on the way, I said to myself, "Maybe he's gone, and I didn't hear the Holy Spirit correctly, or maybe You just wanted to see if I'd really do it like Abraham, putting Isaac up for sacrifice."

Nope, I got there, and he was not at the entrance, but I found him at the exit. I beeped my horn and said, "Hi, remember me from Dunkin' Donuts?" He tilted his head because I was in a different vehicle. "Here's some money, get yourself some food, and have a Merry Christmas." He looked at the $20 dollar bill like it was gold. With tears in his eyes and mine, he said, "Thank you, thank you so much, and God Bless." Isn't it worth it to make someone else's day? It doesn't have to take a lot.

As I am writing this paragraph, this week I saw Charlie again, this time at Kohls. He showed me his humongous stomach hernia and how his boss was out $8,000 due to the electricity wasn't up to code or something. But now his boss has to sue for the money, and he doesn't have any money again. He told me how he had lived off of his mother's estate money, and now he is ineligible for Medicaid or social services. I advised him to go to the hospital and have it taken care of. That's when he told me about not having any insurance. I told him to go, anyway.

He said, "So, it's really hopeless, you see."

I told him, "With God, nothing is hopeless. You just have to believe."

After I had heard his story, I handed him whatever I had in my pocketbook.

He said, "Thank you and thank you for listening to my story. It felt good to get it off my chest."

I said, "You're welcome."

And he said, "God Bless You."

He was gone when I left the store. I did see Charlie one more time when I was close to finishing my book, this time at King Kullen, and he was just standing there, stating he was hungry. I gave him some money, and he thanked me and said, "God bless," and he was gone by the time I left the store. After I finished this book, I never saw Charlie again.

One day I was scheduled to see a woman who was married to another woman. I said to myself, "She is a child of God, and I will treat her with respect and dignity." I'm not here to pass condemnation or to judge her. We talked, and she told me about her chromesthesia (hearing sound and seeing an automatic color). She had Synesthesia, which only 3–5 percent of the population have.[61] It is a neurological phenomenon in which stimulation of one sensory or cognitive pathway leads to automatic, involuntary experiences of a second sensory or cognitive pathway.[62] And no, they are not psychotic, schizophrenic, or delusional. She told me that my voice was like an orange, and her significant other was blue. I had heard of this before but had never ever met anyone who actually had it, and I found it fascinating. Then she told me about her angels and how she can see them at times. Now, she had my full attention. I'm a big, big angel believer and probably watched every episode of "Touched by an Angel" with Roma Downey and Della Reese.[63] She said that one of her angels was wearing a denim cap and blue jeans when she and her significant other were at a horse farm. She said that her angel warned her to step out of the way, and she thought, *Why, this horse is docile enough.* Just then, another horse came by and kicked its hind legs out in her direction. If she hadn't heeded the angel's warning, she could have been dead or severely injured.

I said, "That is very interesting."

---

61 "Synesthesia." 2020. Psychology Today. 2020. https://www.psychologytoday.com/us/basics/synesthesia.
62 Ibid.
63 Touched by An Angel, an American fantasy drama TV series on CBS, 1994–2003 with Roma Downey, Della Reese, and John Dye, created by John Masius (www.wikipedia.org).

She knew the reason for my visit, and she said, "So, do you think I am crazy?"

I said, "No, I believe anything is possible with God. I think it is a gift."

She then said, "I have a message for you from your angels. Would you like to know what it is?"

I was intrigued. I said, "Of course."

She said, "They do not think that you thank them enough."

I said, "That is absolutely true!"

Every time I've had a near car accident and I've had many, or thought I would not make it in time. They have carried me on eagles' wings and gotten me safely and timely (especially in the snowstorms) to my destination. I did see her again to see how she was coping with her G-tube feedings, and she was OK. I gave her a parting gift, which was an angel who lit up in all different colors one at a time. I thought it the perfect Christmas gift for the one who sees and hears in colors and who sees angels and interprets their messages! Now, every time I have a near-miss car accident, I say out loud, "Thank you, Angels. Thank you, God, for sending me an angel." So, you see, God works through people that you would never imagine He would.

So, yes, angels live amongst us today. We, the nurses, have always said that this one nurse, Judy, that we worked with, "had an angel on her shoulder." She would put herself in harm's way, trying to talk down a psychotic, violent patient and come away unscathed. Or the time she was in a blizzard, her car broke down and it was 1 a.m. coming home from work, everyone was told to stay home due to it was declared a state of emergency. It was dark with no cars on the road. The snow was knee-high, and she was alone. She could do nothing but wait, for she didn't have her cell phone on her. A little while later (before she froze to death), she saw a truck driver with a snowplow, she waved him down, and he gave her a ride home. (I really think he was an angel.)

I was sent to this biker's house because he lost his left leg in a motorcycle accident, an above the knee amputation. I was there to see how he was coping from losing his leg, the phantom pains and the real pains, whether he was depressed from losing his leg, and having any PTSD, anger issues, or what exactly he was feeling. Being involved with bikers myself, in my early twenties, I knew how important losing his motorcycle, a Harley Davidson (it was totaled), was to the man who rides one.

So, I go expecting the worst, asking the Holy Spirit to give me whatever necessary words I may have to speak to console him. But to my amazement, he is in good spirits, sitting at the table in his wheelchair, having breakfast. After we make cordial conversation about biker bars, charity runs, Harley Davidson's, I tell him I'm there for two reasons. One to check his healing by rewrapping his stump (the part of his leg that is still there), and two to see how he's adjusting to losing his bike and his leg.

He now knows I'm on the same page as him, and I'm really there to help. I rewrap his stump as he tells me about the accident and how his Harley is totaled, and how the insurance company is coming today to give an estimate of the price they will pay him. Then he tells me an interesting story. He says, "If it weren't for those two angels, whoever they were, who put that tourniquet around my leg at the scene of the accident and who called 911, I'd be dead right now. I thank God I'm here to tell you my story, and on top of that, the insurance guy will give me enough to buy another bike, and with my prosthetic leg, I will ride again!" I said, "Good for You," and when he showed me the mangled bike in the garage, he wasn't kidding. He really did have angels watching over him. I never expected it to go as well as it had. Expect the unexpected with God.

My friend, Renuka, told me recently that she was sitting at a red light, and she could see in her rearview mirror a car that was barreling down the road and was not going to stop in time before it got to her. She just closed her eyes and said, "Oh, my Jesus." With that, the car careened around her, and she was saved from any harm. She told me she knew it was divine intervention that God must have sent an angel to guard her against harm.

God speaks to us by answering our prayers. Sometimes we have to ask in prayer with a pure heart for the things we need or want. But that's in another chapter.

And strangely enough, God speaks to us through our pain. Pain is the fifth vital sign, as we nurses' put it. It signals something is wrong, i.e., heart attack. When you're in severe physical pain, nothing else matters but for it to subside. Some try to pray it away, while others say, "To hell with God."

Those of us who pray it away, pray for courage and strength to endure it as well as asking for it to subside. Sometimes we ask, "For what purpose does this serve, Lord?" But the Lord does not give us more than we can handle. Jesus was a carpenter/craftsman. He knows his kinds of wood: oak, pine, maple. He knows about size, depth, height, and weight of each. He also knows, as should we, that our cross would never be any more than we can bear. And yes, we may fall, once, twice, three times, or more in this life before we get to our heavenly destination. That being said, we come out on the other side by grace.

I've asked, "What is it I need to work on this time, Lord? Trust, patience, humility, gratitude? And I know there is always the *light* at the end of the tunnel. His *light* for He is the light of the world. The *light* that I will see at the end of my life. Whether it is physical or emotional pain, we all walk through our storms by grace. "Faith isn't flying above the storm; it's weathering the storm," I heard a pastor say.

Pain isn't always a negative connotation. It's God's way of getting our attention. Jesus said that we will have trials and tribulations in this world (Romans 5:3). It's in that pain stemming from our trials and tribulations, which opens the door to humility, our alone time with our Creator—the questioning and sometimes even the answers. The slowing down of time, slowing enough to stop and listen to what He wants from us and for us. It's the intimate time of knowing that He can take it all away in a blink of an eye. It is the reason to enjoy the here and now. It's the where with all to find Joy in the moment and to appreciate what you have rather than what you do not. It's the revelation that He is in control, and we are not.

Pain has a way of bringing us back to reality and bringing us to our knees. Sometimes it's a good thing, a needed thing; a reminder that there is something greater than ourselves. Pain builds faith, perseverance, hope, which builds a bridge between ourselves and God the Almighty. There is a reason for everything God does and a season under heaven. Jesus said, "And behold,

I am with you always, until the end of age" (Matthew 28:20 NABRE).

Pain reflects things accomplished and mirrors things yet to come. Pain opens the door to love; pain entertains the possibilities of Hope; it invades our inner being. Pain teaches us patience and reliance on others. Some believe that pain is a pursuit of a Godly goal, as evidenced by the cross. Believe me; God gets it. Jesus experienced pain (the whipping at the post with cat-of-nine-tails, and the nailing to the cross), betrayal by Judas, anger in the temple with the sellers. He experienced sorrow and grief when his good friend died. It states, "Jesus wept" when He came to his friend Lazarus' tomb. He experienced hunger, thirst, and tiredness when he was fasting in the wilderness for forty days and nights, and even some doubt... "Lord if it be thy will, take this cup from me" (Luke 22:42 NLT). He endured it all for us. During my pain, both the physical and emotional facets of pain, it has brought me closer to God. The closer you move towards God, the closer He moves towards you (James 4:8).

With my home care nursing job, in the privacy of their homes, people felt more comfortable opening up about their doubts, fears, anxieties, and thoughts without any judgment or repercussions. Sometimes, they just needed to get it off their chest, tell a professional, or just hear it said out loud. Before I left many of them,

I knew that person's life story, struggles, accomplishments as well as failures and an interpersonal connection was made. I would remind them about the "good" that came from their life, giving them praise and encouragement and acceptance, and sometimes I'd suggest an antidepressant and/or therapist. I would pray before entering each new home that the Holy Spirit would give me the insight and understanding, strength and courage needed to help His children. Because at the end of the day, no matter what faith you are, you are still a child of God.

I had a friend that I worked with and attended church with who was so busy with work and church activities, she barely had time for herself or her family. She had adopted two boys, one was handicapped. He was simply so loveable. One day she broke her ankle and had to slow down. She came to work in a cast. Although it was painful, I said to her, "Don't you think God is trying to tell you something? "He's trying to tell you to slow down and spend some time with your family, especially Tommy." She said, "I think you're right; Tommy was so happy to have me lie on the couch and just watch TV with him." Sometimes so simple yet so obvious a message.

Many people have real physical pain and need medication for it. That's a fact. With my first hip surgery, I had excruciating pain, and it seemed worse at night—

All alone in the dark. I couldn't take opiates because they made me sick, so another six hours before I could get some Tylenol, I thought I was going to die. I learned to trust. Inspired by Max Lucado's book *Unshakable Hope*, I wrote:

*Dear Lord,*

*As your daughter, I am thankful for All you have given me.*

*I realize my suffering here on earth is nothing compared to Jesus' suffering on that cross.*

*For I know that All things work out for our Good to those called by God (chosen ones) (Romans 8:28).*

*With the strength of the Holy Spirit's guidance, may I find my true joy, true peace, and true love in your Son, Jesus Christ.*

*Amen.*

A professor once said, "That Psychology means the medical healing of the soul." I went into psychiatry nursing because I feel that for a person to heal from whatever ailment they have, it needs to come from their mind, body, and soul—the Spirit of God, not just their body. I encourage them to choose life, choose joy. C. S. Lewis said, "God whispers to us in our pleasures, speaks in our conscience, but shouts in our pains: it is His megaphone to rouse a deaf world..."[64]

---

64 "Quote by C.S. Lewis." n.d. Goodreads, Inc. 2020. https://www. goodreads.com/quotes/623193-we-can-ignore-even-pleasure-but-pain-insists-upon-being.

# CHAPTER 7

# Miracles Abound

My God is a God of miracles! He said, "Let there be light..." and he created the heavens and the earth, separated the day and the night, the sun and the stars (Genesis 1:3 NIV, 2:1; 1:16). He took dirt and breathed life into it and made Adam (Genesis 2:7). God had Gideon down to 300 men for battling of 135,000 men, and with faith, they won without ever lifting a sword (Judges 7:16, 8:10, 7:22).

God parted the Red Sea so that approximately two million Israelites could walk through, and he fed them manna from heaven for 40 years (Exodus 12:37, 14:22, 16:4).

My God told the prophet, Elijah, to pour four large jars of water on the altar before He sets the offering ablaze (1 Kings 18:33). Elijah must have thought, *Really? You must really want to make your point, God.* The 450 priests with their infidel god Baal could not even make a spark come from their offerings (1 Kings 18:19, 29).

And it was Jesus who turned water into wine, calmed the sea, healed the sick with just His words as with the centurion's servant, or by her just touching His cloak she was healed from twelve years of hemorrhaging (John 2:9; Mark 4:39; Matthew 8:13, 9:20, 22). He cast out many demons and made them go into pigs and run off a cliff (Matthew 8:31, 32). He cured a blind man with just his spittle (Mark 8:23, 25). He was crucified and died and rose again and appeared to hundreds (Mark 25:25, 16:6; Acts1:3). Death no longer has any power over us. This is our miracle.

Miracles still happen in today's world. Just look around. You just have to be aware that they do indeed exist. You are a miracle. God made you with an infinite number of cells carrying out precise functions of breathing, carrying oxygen, pumping blood to and from your heart to each muscle cell, coordinating the movements of your hands, legs, feet, eyes, heart, and diaphragm. Your nerve cells controlling our senses and ability to feel sensations. You are a walking, talking, seeing, breathing, heart-pumping miracle. Each unique with our own set of DNA molecules! So, don't let anyone say, "I've never seen a miracle."

Have you ever looked in the mirror lately or at another human being? What about the beauty of creation? Every day the sun rises, and the sunsets; the moon and the stars come out each night; the coming in and going out of the tides; the innumerable, yet distinctly different amount of colors, species, as well as sizes and shapes of fish in the Great Barrier Reef in Australia, which I personally have witnessed.

I wondered if God has a sense of humor and had not created each unique fish to correspond to each individual human on earth. We are fearfully and wonderfully made! (Psalms 139:14) Have you ever seen a sunrise or sunset, heard the sound of birds chirping in the morning air, or the sound of a newborn baby's cry? Watched the wings of the butterfly dance across the sky, or the endless breaking of the waves of the ocean upon its shores? Or witnessed the infinite counting of stars in the sky? Nature, in all its wonder and splendor in which we, who are beautifully and fearfully made in His im-

age, are privileged to live in. Every day you live and
breathe is God's miracle to you. Remember, He said,
"Before I formed you in the womb I knew you..." (Jeremiah 1:5 NIV). I know every hair on your head (Luke
12:7). When I stop to look at what the Master has done,
I'm in awe. As I was watching the Great Barrier Reef on
my computer screen, I wrote:

> *Watching all the numerous creatures both*
> *great and small and*
> > *The perfect diversity amongst them all*
> > *Only God could have accomplished this Beauty*
> *in*
> > *All of this underwater ocean,*
> > *How much more intricately and perfect*
> > *Did He create mankind?*
> > *We are made in His image,*
> > *Both Beautifully*
> > *and Wonderfully made.*

I will take the everyday mundane miracles. I don't
need to walk on water like St. Peter did (Matthew 14:29).
I don't need to feed 5,000 people with just five loaves
and two fishes, heal the sick, cast out demons, or give
sight to the blind (Matthew 14:19–21, 17:18, 15:31). But
you do need to learn not to miss the smaller ones so that
you will surely not miss the larger ones.

What is a miracle really? A miracle is defined as a surprising and welcomed event that is not explicable by natural or scientific laws and is therefore considered to be the work of a divine agency; an unusual or wonderful event that is believed to be caused by the power of God.[65]

I believe miracles abound; we just don't stop and look, listen, and process things that happen that way. But I do happen to be among the few that do. I'll share with you what I consider to be miracles.

I was working the day shift at the hospital driving my 2002 Mercury Mountaineer, a forty-five-minute drive on the expressway doing sixty-five miles an hour. As I was backing into a parking spot, I heard a crunch and a thump, and my front axle and my tire fell off! I was aghast! I thought, *Oh God, I'll need a tow truck, another expense that I could not afford.* I now had to be late to work, call Security police because I was half in the parking space and half out of the space blocking anyone from getting to or from. When the policeman came and sized up the extent of the damage, he said, "You are so lucky that the tire didn't fly off the axle on your way here at sixty-five mph you would have been dead." I never thought of that. I knew it wasn't luck; it was my God whom I prayed to on my way to work. He sent His

---

65 "Miracle." n.d. Oxford Reference. 2020. https://www.oxfordreference.com/view/10.1093/oi/authority.20110803100200612.

angels to protect me. This was one of my miracles. As was written in a prior chapter, my other miracles were when my son Jonathan did not fall off the mountainside in Panama, and when my son Ronnie was exonerated of all that had happened at college.

A few years later, my eldest son, Ronnie, was doing seventy mph on the highway when he ran something over, and it put a hole in his rim. He moved the car from the third lane to the side of the road without hitting anyone nor anyone hitting him. A Department of transportation worker assisted him with the changing of the tire. He then said, "You're lucky, if that piece of metal kept going through into the car, your legs would have been cut off!" I told my unbelieving son that "It was a miracle you weren't killed or maimed!" This was definitely a divine intervention for sure.

My friend, Loretta's oldest daughter, had gotten herself into drugs. Heroin, to be exact. For approximately twelve years, Loretta would go months at a time, not knowing whether her daughter was dead or alive. She would call or text with no response. For about five years, Loretta would go down to Delaware to search for her among the homeless, getting clues from her last job or methadone clinic. She would always find her, which in itself was a miracle. Then she'd help her with a place to live or a good meal and some clothes. She let her daughter know that she was always loved and prayed for but could not come home until she gave up the drugs. Loretta would always pray for her, and she never gave up hope even in ten years. Then Loretta started fasting. One day she heard from her daughter, who declared that she was done with drugs. She was tapering herself off methadone and going through the withdrawal alone with the headaches, nausea, and vomiting; she did it! At age thirty-something, she was now ready to come home. Loretta had heard of a half-way house for her to go to while attending a rehab program not far from her home. Her daughter, now, came home. This is Loretta's miracle.

In Rabbi Jonathan Cahn's book *The Harbinger*, he reports that St. Paul's Chapel was protected by a sycamore tree, which was the only building left standing at 9/11.[66] This was the place the United States prayed on the first inauguration day of President George Washington. Coincidence? I think not. I believe Cahn warns us that this terrorist attack is a warning for America to repent before it is destroyed, just like ancient Israel was. How can it be explained about the steel that was left standing in the formation of a huge cross? Or about the people that were late or didn't go to work at the Trade Center that day? This is their miracle.

---

66 Cahn, Jonathan. 2012. The Harbinger: The Ancient Mystery That Holds the Secret of America's Future. Frontline.

What about the book *Unbroken* by Laura Hillenbrand and the movie *Unbroken: Path of Redemption*, where Louis Zamperini, the gold medal Olympic winner, was adrift on a raft after being shot down by enemy planes for days.[67] Out of nowhere, a seagull lands on his raft after they have been without food for thirty days. He then spends months in a Japanese torture camp by the cruelest of Japanese guards. When he comes home to the United States, he marries, but he screams in his sleep, having vivid nightmares of the Prisoner of War (POW) camp that haunts him. He self-medicates (post-traumatic stress disorder wasn't even a disorder at that time) with alcohol. His wife was on the verge of divorcing him when she begged him to go see Billy Graham with her. Billy Graham was speaking in the tent in California in 1949.[68] Just to placate her, he went... both he and his marriage were "saved" that night. He had forgotten that he prayed every day and night while he was in that Japanese prison camp. He states, "I stopped drinking and never had another nightmare again."[69]

God is always doing miracles for us every day behind the scenes, even! You can hear about someone getting cured of an illness just about every day if you listen to

---

67 "Unbroken (Film) - Wikipedia." 2020. *Wikipedia, The Free Encyclopedia.* 2020. https://en.wikipedia.org/wiki/Unbroken_(film).
68 Billy Graham 's Los Angeles Crusade 1949-his first great evangelistic campaign lasted for eight weeks.
69 "Unbroken (Film) - Wikipedia." 2020.

a preacher on Television, somewhere in the world the fact that we have Trinity Broadcasting Network (TBN) started by Jan and Paul Crouch and Eternal Word Television Network (EWTN) that Mother Angelica started is on TV 24 hours a day, seven days a week, around the world, is in itself, a miracle.

Two of my friends read their Bibles every day and prayed diligently. They both pray for their children and spouses to know the Lord. They have been praying for about twenty years. One day one of my friend's husband went with her to a religious conference. He was touched by the Holy Spirit and was saved! Never give up on prayer. This proved to my other friend that there is always hope in prayer. It is the strongest weapon we have against the devil. Many say that prayer is love in action. You may say, "Well, what can I do?" "Praying" is the answer! As St. Paul said, "We must pray unceasingly" (1 Thessalonians 5:17).

As with Immaculee' Ilibagiza in her book, *Left to Tell*, she talks about discovering God during the 1994 Rwandan genocide as she and her brother were the only ones spared in her family.[70] She was left to tell the story of how a pastor took her and seven other women and hid them in a tiny bathroom behind a wardrobe for approximately ninety days. She said that she prayed from 6 a.m.–9

---

70 Immaculee Ilibagiza. 2006. Left to Tell: Discovering God Amidst the Rwandan Holocaust. Hay House.

p.m., and she held onto the rosary her father gave her and prayed day and night in the three-foot by four-foot bathroom.[71] The fear was overwhelming. She could hear the killers (Hudu's) yelling her name with their machetes in hand, and if they found her, they would surely kill her. They butchered her family. Approximately 1 million Tutsis were murdered in 100 days. Not only is her life a testimony to how powerful our God is and the miracle that Immaculee encountered but also of the power that prayer has. Never underestimate the power of prayer!

There's the story of Desmond Doss, the private who refused to carry a rifle, and they attempted to court-martial him in the movie *Hacksaw Ridge* (a true story).[72] He strictly believed that "Thou shall not kill" under any circumstances (he was a 7th Day Adventist Christian). He was also ridiculed and beaten and called "a coward" by fellow soldiers for this. During the fighting on that ridge, the Americans were told to retreat because they were being overcome by the Japanese. He, single-handedly, without a weapon, went back to save over seventy-five wounded American troops from behind enemy lines off that ridge![73] Some men have attested, "If it weren't for Doss, I would have died that day."[74]

---

71 Ilibagiza. 2006.
72 "Hacksaw Ridge." 2020. *Wikipedia, The Free Encyclopedia.* https://en.wikipedia.org/wiki/Hacksaw_Ridge.
73 Ibid.
74 Ibid.

There's no way one man of his own accord could have done all that, without the help of God Almighty and His army of angels! That's God working His miracle behind the scenes.

I just heard last night, on the news, that a seventy-four-year-old lady in India had given birth to twins via in vitro fertilization (IVF) and her eighty-two-year-old husband said, "We've always wanted to have children."[75] That's surely a miracle.

My sister Christine has had her miracles as well. Almost two weeks to the day, after she had gotten her phone, she called to say that she was contemplating going to the ER because of severe lower right quadrant abdominal pain for four days. I said, "GO! You could have a ruptured appendix; you could die." She was hesitant because she did not know how she would be able to pay for it. She calls her job to tell them, and the supervisor told her, "You have been here six months to the day, and you are entitled to one weeks' vacation with pay!"

Thank God because she lives paycheck to paycheck, and it turns out she needed it. Sure enough, she did have to get an emergency appendectomy. The doctor said he would not know if it was ruptured or not until he opened her up. Prayers were offered from my Bible

75  Tan, Rebecca, and Tania Dutta. 2019. "74-Year-Old Mangay-amma Yaramati Gives Birth to Twins in India." The Washington Post. 2019. https://www.washingtonpost.com/world/2019/09/06/this-year-old-woman-just-gave-birth-twins/.

group as well as myself that it was not ruptured. It was not ruptured, which is a miracle in itself. But the fact that she could communicate with me and let me know she had left the OR and was in recovery was a God send. Since she lived four hours away, I could not get there in time if I had tried. She was discharged three days later, and my eldest brother and I went to pick her up from the hospital and get her the necessary items she needed, i.e., pain medications and food. She then found out that there was a charitable organization that paid for her whole hospital stay, all $25,000! This was truly a blessing from God! These are her miracles.

In the book, *Girl With No Name* by Marina Chapman, who in 1954 was abducted when she was about four-years-old, was dragged into the jungle, molested, and left to die.[76] She did not die; she was raised by capuchin monkeys who took her in as one of their own. Talk about God's providence! Until found by hunters and sold to a brothel, she believed she was a monkey. She did escape, and according to Pastor Jentezen Franklin on TBN, she is a Christian today. This is her miracle.

I was paying for something I bought at the Shrine's gift store when the man behind the counter started to tell me his story. He said, "I was in a motorcycle acci-

---

76 Chapman, Marina. 2013. *The Girl With No Name: The Incredible True Story of a Child Raised by Monkeys*. Pegasus. https://www.goodreads.com/book/show/16102341-the-girl-with-no-name.

dent at age seventeen and was in a coma for two and a half months with brain hemorrhages. I've been coming to this church for twenty-three years now. Don't forget what God can do. I was paralyzed on my left side, and now I can ride again." "Wow, that is a miraculous story," I told him.

You just have to believe. If you don't believe, you will never see a miracle. Expect the unexpected. It's those "Ah-hah" moments that you will see when you do. Step out of the boat with your faith so that He can make the leap of faith needed to make your miracle happen. When you cannot do it with your own strength, that's when God steps in and performs a miracle. There are miracles all around us. You just have to know where and how to look to see it.

There is this Television show called *God Friended Me*.[77] It's about a friend suggestion forwarded to Miles, an atheist, on social media from God. Miles doesn't believe God sent it and attempts to find the culprit. But in the midst of all of this, you see how intertwined people's lives really are. Miles' father is a pastor; his mother was killed by a drunk driver after having beat cancer. Miles was very young at the time, and so was his sister. His first friend's suggestion is a man who attempts to kill himself by throwing himself in front of a subway.

---

77 "God Friended Me." 2020. *Wikipedia, The Free Encyclopedia.* 2020. https://en.wikipedia.org/wiki/God_Friended_Me.

After Miles saves him, his next friend's suggestion is a young girl named Cara. She is hit by a car in the middle of a traffic jam, Miles yells, "Help! Is there a doctor?" Out of a N.Y. city yellow cab comes the man from the subway who is a doctor. Cara becomes his girlfriend. All the people they meet and the reasons for helping them, and how each person is related to another is truly divine. I know it has to be God behind the online account. I mean, why not? God has used a lot of stranger things, like a burning bush, why isn't it feasible that He would use modern technology to get his message across to the people of today? I like the concept of this show and the realities of the peoples' lives and how they are all interrelated. And it's ironic that God chose an atheist to help see God's hand in all of these people's lives.

Albert Einstein once said, "There are only two ways to live your life. One is as though nothing is a miracle. The other is as though everything is a miracle."[78]

I recently read Mark Batterson's book *Circle Maker* and how he and his wife wanted to buy a house, but their offer was refused.[79] They accepted it as God's will. One year later, he testifies that the same house was tak-

78 "Quote by Albert Einstein." n.d. Goodreads, Inc. 2020. https:// www.goodreads.com/quotes/987-there-are-only-two-ways-to-live-your-life-one.
79 Batterson, Mark. 2016. *The Circle Maker.* Zondervan. https://www.christianbook.com/the-circle-maker-mark-batterson/9780310346913/pd/346913.

en off the market and now was up for sale again, and this time, the buyer accepted their same offer. They were able to sell their house for more than what they would have gotten for it a year ago. That's how God moves when you believe. You have to acknowledge the little miracles and blessings before He can give you the larger ones. Become open to Him and His blessings and grace.

They say, "Count your blessings." A blessing could be a special favor or gift from God. I thank God every day for the many blessings He has given me—My children, my family, my friends, my home, etc.

I remember a freezing evening in November. I went to King Kullen for something. And I usually never go to KK. I usually go to another supermarket. As I pulled into the parking lot, I saw what appeared to be a Middle Eastern family sitting on the cold curb. A mother with a scarf around her head holding an infant, two girls with scarves around their heads, and a young boy and a father holding up a sign, "No Job Please HELP."

I parked my car and jumped out and yelled at him, "What are you doing?" pointing to his family freezing on the curb.

He said, "I lost my contracting job at Home Depot, and now I am short on rent money."

I said, "Do you have a place to live?"

He said, "Yes."

I said, "So, go on unemployment."

He replied, "I cannot. We are illegal refugees".

I thought, *OH, my God, U.S. Immigration and Customs Enforcement (ICE) will have a field day with this!* I asked, "Do you have a place to stay?"

He said, "Yes."

I gave them some money and prayed for them. I gave them half of what I had in my pocket, and he said, "God Bless," and then I noticed other cars were stopping and giving money too. I wanted to tell them to get off the street before ICE comes and takes them all away. As I wandered the store, I thought maybe I should be buying them some food, but I did not know what they would eat or what facilities they had where they lived. When I came out of the store, they were gone. Hopefully to somewhere safe.

I've heard it said, "Count your blessings," but what is a Blessing? Special favor, mercy, or benefit: "The act or words of a person who blesses. A favor or gift bestowed by God, thereby bringing happiness. The invoking of God's favor upon a person."[80] Be a blessing to someone else. It can be as simple as lending an ear to listen to a lonely person, giving someone a ride to work or church, showing concern or compassion, giving of our time or money to help someone out.

---

80 "Definition of Blessing." 2020. Dictionary.Com. 2020. https://www.dictionary.com/browse/blessing?s=t.

I count my blessings all the time; my children, family, friends, home, etc. For some it's hearing their baby's first cry, or for some, it's affording the house they've been praying for or their car. For others, it's getting the job they've always wanted, being able to provide for their family, and for others, it is simply having a roof over their head and food on their table. Sometimes it's the blessing from their priest or pastor over them or their religious article. I truly believe God blesses us when we bless others, a thought shared by many. Bless someone by buying school supplies for the needy or food /shelter for the homeless, or giving your excess cans of food to the church pantry. Indirectly you are being that person's miracle. It may even save a life. We have to give with your heart, not your head, and God will multiply your gifts with His power. Do not give to see what your reward will be or how this will benefit me. "Give to Give, not Give to Get," as I heard Pastor Robert Morris say.[81]

I had just finished reading a fiction book called the *Homeless Bishop* by Joseph F. Girzone. And coincidently enough, Jesus was homeless as well as His disciples, moving around from town to town spreading the Good News, staying with friendly strangers who would take them in and give them food. While I was in Best Market, I saw a man ahead of me in line, disheveled look-

81 "Robert Morris, Gateway Church (Texas)." 2020.

ing, dressed in layers with old worn clothing. He had a small brown bag in one hand, which could have been a bottle of alcohol. He had only three items on the counter, some bread and cold cuts for a sandwich and some pickles and a jar of peppers—Things that needed no refrigeration. He was quite unkept, unshaven, unclean, and I surmised that he was homeless. It was very cold out, and a blizzard was coming. I intuitively heard that still small voice say, "Pay for his things." *Maybe he could use his money for a place to stay the night instead,* I thought.

I approached the man very gingerly and softly asked him, "Do you mind if I pay for your items and just let her ring it up with mine? It's called paying it forward." The man acted like he had won the lottery!

He said, "Really? I saw that movie and have always tried to; it has never been done to me!"

I said, "Well, now it's your turn. Go with God."

He said, "Thank you. Thank you."

I said, "You are welcome."

Then he followed me out of the store and asked me, "What's your name?"

I said, "Laura."

He said, "I'm Tony, thank you, Laura," and we parted ways.

I wondered where he would stay that night. I said a little prayer for him. I heard a man interviewed on the news recently after he had left some food on a man's doorstep, he said, "When you do something good for someone else, yeah, they benefit from it but, you really do it for "you". I thought, *How profound, how true that statement really is.*

My son Ronnie was giving his drum set to his cousin because he seldom used it any more. I couldn't afford lessons any longer. It was a $500 drum set in fair condition. When my brother came to take the drum set, he handed my son a $100 bill. My son was very happy because he wasn't expecting anything and that was a lot of money for him at the time. God sees your heart.

One winter day back in the early 1990s, I was in Toys R Us, and I had very little money to spend on the boys that Christmas. I was trying to decide what was the most important when I looked down at the floor, to my surprise, I saw a $100 bill! I thought I had hit the lottery! But reality set in, and my first thought was that someone had dropped it and would come looking for it. I hung around to see if someone would come to look for it or if an announcement would come overhead. Nothing. I thought, *Should I go to the desk and tell them?* My son said, "If you go there and give them the $100 bill, you will never see it again." He had a point. There are not that many honest people left in the world. I took it as a blessing from God and thanked Him, and bought extra things for my boys that I didn't originally have the money for.

Twice I was called to see a Muslim patient. We are all God's children, and I treated him as such. This man owned his own taxi company. I was called to see him because he was a victim of violence. His wife was present and his two children. He was badly beaten while driving two men in his taxi. For no other reason than he was a Muslim, they beat him so badly he now had a traumatic brain injury and possibly would lose the sight in his right eye. He was devastated and depressed.

It is now Christmas time, and they have no income. The social worker contacted the local mosque to make them aware, but now they were too ashamed. They did not want the community to know. His wife told me that they say "Merry Christmas" to non-Muslim friends. She also told me that they are struggling financially because he was the only one who worked in the family. They did not know how they were going to pay for food, rent, their two school-age children's needs, and other bills. I heard the Holy Spirit tell me to buy a $100 gift card to Best Yet market for them. Twice they had not accepted my visit, but on my third attempt, they did agree to see me. He was feeling a little better. Someone was helping him to run his business. As I left for the last time, I slipped the gift card into the wife's pocket and said, "Merry Christmas," and departed. I wanted to send a message that there is more to Christianity.

I remember one man I visited a couple of days before Thanksgiving. And he was just released from the hospital after having a quadruple bypass. He had just started a new job and was out of work for five months prior. He had two sons and a mentally ill sister living with him. His wife walked away four years ago. He got home and found out that his car was repossessed. He had borrowed money and had obtained a ride to pay the $2,000 for his car, but when he got to the Department of Motor Vehicles (DMV) for his plates, they wanted $780 more!

His blood pressure was running high, as could be expected. He could not get to the store without a vehicle. When his sister opened the refrigerator, I could see there was nothing but a half-gallon of milk inside. He was at the end of his rope. He was frantically looking online on how to borrow money. I asked him what his plans were for Thanksgiving, and he said that he did not have any. He had no money, no car, and now, they were threatening to shut off his electricity.

When I left, I called the social worker and asked if we could get him a food voucher and if she could bump him up on the priority list. I could buy some food for Thanksgiving and leave it on his doorstep. I remember the joy it brought our family when we received such a basket from the local church for Thanksgiving and/or Christmas. It was time to give back. But she said that she had already brought food over. I said, "Thank you, God bless you. Have a wonderful Thanksgiving." God did say to feed the poor (Proverbs 22:9).

It was the day before Easter, and I was in line at Walmart. There was a Spanish woman holding an infant in her arms with a ten-year-old boy. She did not speak English. He was her translator. I saw she had a few items for the baby, diapers and wipes and formula, a package of hot dogs (probably dinner), and some rolls. She put her card through, and it was denied. She did it again, and the cashier told the son it was denied again. She got on her flip phone and made a call. She was holding up the line now. The boy was embarrassed. I was feeling that kid's pain when I heard that still, small voice say, "Pay for her things." As she put her card through a second time, I thought, *Oh, it will work this time, and that will be that.* But it didn't.

I said to the cashier, "Just ring it up with mine, don't worry about it."

So, the cashier said, "OK."

The lady left with the few items, and the boy was translating what had just transpired to his mother when the lady came running over and said in English, "Thank You."

I said, "You are welcome."

The man behind me said to me, "Did you just do what I think you did?"

She said, "Like what?"

I said, "Did you start tithing again?"

She said, "I did."

She started again after her surgery, not expecting anything in return, and God did all these amazing things for her because she did. She stepped out in faith knowing that God would provide for her when she returned to her home without a job, no money in the bank, no credit cards, and a twelve-year-old car.

She said, 'I knew He wouldn't let me starve." She learned to *Live Outside the Box* with just her faith.

"It's all His money anyway," I heard many a pastor say. Just as everything on earth belongs to God, not us, and we cannot take it with us when we die. I remember Fr. J. say, "You will never see a U-Haul truck behind a hearse."

I truly believe God rewards those who do good for the sake of doing good. I have never shared those stories of giving before. It has always been between the Lord and me. I'm sharing them now not to show what a good Christian I am but to make my point.

I am very well aware of my blessings. Like when I got the house, the kids and my pension in the divorce. All he got was his new girlfriend.

When I landed my home care job, it was February 12, the same day, eight years prior that my husband had left us. I remember running out of oil that night, and the boys and I slept together in the living room with the fireplace on to keep warm. I didn't have the money for fuel oil. And the fact that it was two days before Valentine's day, I was completely distraught. But with the grace of God, I now have enough. Our God knows and sees our needs, and He provides for us.

I remember the time my ex-husband had promised me that on my fiftieth birthday, he would buy me a new red convertible Seabring. All I got was divorce papers. Some twelve years later, after church, I drove to a Chevy Cadillac dealership to look at new cars. My lease with KIA was almost up, and I was curious about what was new on the market. I always said jokingly, "When I retire, I'm going to get a Cadillac." It was more of a dream rather than reality, so I had thought. To my surprise, I leased a new red Cadillac SUV. As I was driving home in it, I realized it was April 30, 2018. This would have been my thirtieth wedding anniversary. God can even make dreams come true.

And sometimes, the bad thing that happens to you is His blessing in disguise. Like the time, my friend Renuka wanted to work per diem as a nurse at her hospice home care job. She wanted me to help her with her resume, and I did. Then two weeks before Christmas, the agency let her go. They said she said something she never said (she had worked there twenty-four years).

She told them, "You know my work ethics, but you have yourself a very Merry Christmas." She felt a peace about it. She thought about suing them for defamation of character but decided it was a blessing in disguise because she did not want to work there any longer, but her husband wasn't too keen on her leaving. After approximately a month or so, she thought it was somewhat boring, and I told her to trust God. "He has something bigger and better in store for you." She got involved in her church, and God called her to be a deaconess and a biblical counselor. She could never have done these things while working.

Another one of my friends, Judy, was retired and working full time at another hospital. They let her go for some ridiculous reason. And I told her it probably was a blessing in disguise, and it was. She now had more time to spend with her grandchildren.

When I didn't get the job, I casually wanted after I left my home care job, it was a blessing in disguise for me because I was now there to drive my friend, Tee, for her chemo. We'd talk about God and faith and heaven. I'd tell her about the book I was going to write. We'd talk about the new movies *Paul Apostle of Christ* and *I Can Only Imagine*. We'd listen to *The Message* on Sirius XM while we drove. She said she was afraid to die. I don't know why she was afraid. I don't know if her faith wasn't strong enough, or that she was questioning her relationship with the Lord. I told her that I dreamt I was driving, and my car slid off the bridge, and as I was falling, I saw the trees, the birds, and a waterfall. I said, "Thank you God, for allowing me to see your beautiful creation one last time before I die." I was at peace, I wasn't afraid, but I wasn't the one actively dying either. I was able to be with her because I didn't work. The moral of this story is that God always sees the bigger picture (which we cannot see), and it's always His best plan for you. We can't see the future; we can only see the past and the present.

The guy on the news said, "If you think you're going to have a White Christmas, you'd better pray for a miracle." Christmas was to be at my house this year with my mother and five siblings and their spouses and children, approximately twenty people in all. I was so excited to host Christmas as it is my favorite holiday. I thought it would be nice to have a white Christmas, but I'm not going to pray for that because there are so many more important things to pray for, like peace on earth, the soldiers, my family and friends, my children. I wouldn't want to take up your time just for that, Lord. That morning, December 25, 2013, I awoke, and to my surprise, there was a beautiful white blanket of snow all over the front yard! I was like, You heard my unspoken prayer. You never cease to amaze me. It was the first Christmas at my house in years! The first time I could afford it. The lights looked so pretty against the snow. I had blue and white stars to represent Jesus as *the light of the world* and the stars over Bethlehem. I had little Christmas trees lining the walkway. The first time in eight years that I had a real tree and lights put up by my sons! Again, I was so blessed!

Basic things like food, water, shelter, we have taken for granted, but these are our everyday miracles. There are people in third world countries who do not have clean water to drink, and children die daily because of this. No food nor shelter, America's homeless are a prime example. Some are because of bad breaks, loss of a job, tough situations, or natural catastrophes. We need to embrace them with the grace in which God has shown us.

What exactly is grace? It is God's gift freely given, enabling power and spiritual healing offered through the mercy and love of Jesus Christ.[87]

It's the unmerited favor of God, something unde-served, given freely without us having to ask or beg for. There but for the grace of God go I. When I see a homeless person, I think that could be me, but only for the grace of God, I am not. My brother-in-law told me one day, "You have found favor with the Lord, Laura." I was shocked. I never thought of it like that before. As

---

87 "Grace in Christianity." 2020. *Wikipedia, The Free Encyclopedia.* 2020. https://en.wikipedia.org/wiki/Grace_in_Christianity.

I thought about it, I guess I had. I was still struggling financially and emotionally, but He was still providing. And that is my saving grace story.

I'm sure you are familiar with the song *Amazing Grace*, written by Captain John Newton.[88] He lived a life of debauchery. While at sea, a storm came and threatened to overcome him and his whole crew. He prayed and begged God to save both himself and his crew, and He did. That is an example of what grace did for him.

The time I got a flat tire in my driveway, and I was late for work, I called the number for assistance, and it would be an hour before someone would arrive to fix it. I was somewhat annoyed because now my whole day was backed up. I had to call my supervisor and all my patients for that day and explain what had happened as I waited. When he arrived, a young African American man, I apologized because I do not carry cash, and all I had was a cold bottle of water to offer him.

He graciously accepted it and said, "No worries, if you hadn't have gotten a flat, I wouldn't have had a job today."

I said to him, "So... God is good?"

He replied, "All the time!"

"Amen," I said.

That's the power of grace.

---

88 "Amazing Grace." 2020. *Wikipedia, The Free Encyclopedia*. 2020. https://en.wikipedia.org/wiki/Amazing_Grace.

Sometimes He uses us indirectly to provide grace for someone else.

Another example is the parable of the ninety-nine sheep and the one who was lost. When the one that was lost was found, the shepherd rejoiced (Luke 15:4–6). It was the same with the prodigal son. He was lost then came home, and his father ran to embrace him, and he rejoiced (Luke 15:32). It is the Lord who rejoices when we who are lost come home to Him. Our Father in heaven rejoices and embraces us. He always accepts us back, no matter the circumstances or how long we have been astray. There is no hole deep enough that the Lord cannot reach into and pull us out. And that is Amazing Grace.

I asked God every day to help me care for my patients. To give me the courage and wisdom, knowledge, and strength to care for these people under my care. I prayed. I opened the Bible, and it said, "Because you have not asked for riches or wealth or honor for yourself but for wisdom... I will grant you wisdom, knowledge, long life, honor, and countless riches" (2 Chronicles 1:11, 12). King Solomon was the wisest and the richest man in the world because he had only asked for wisdom.

I've heard it said, "With Grace comes Wisdom." Wisdom comes from the Holy Spirit and is pure. I wrote in my journal:

*All that I am...*
*All that I have...*
*All that I know...*
*All that I see...*
*All that I do...*
*Is but for the grace of God.*


We must humbly admit this to ourselves because we could not have done any of it without His help.

The heart sees, the heart listens, the heart speaks, the heart feels, the heart knows, the heart understands, and the heart believes. You can believe with your mind, but when you believe with your heart, you know that you believe.

The Holy Spirit speaks to your heart, and the heart hears. The word "ear" is in the middle of the word "heart". The Spirit speaks to your heart when you read the printed words of the Bible or when you hear the Word of God. You can feel the Holy Spirit within your heart. The Holy Spirit helps us understand the will of God within our hearts, not our minds. Thus, you can believe in God with your whole heart.

Another example is when you listen to another with your heart, and you feel compassion and empathy. Sometimes no words are even necessary; that is when the heart speaks. That small inner voice, sometimes that is when the Holy Spirit speaks to you... if you listen closely. Here's what I've discovered:

Be Still and Know That I am God

Be still and know that I AM

Be still and Know;

Be Still

Be.

And...

God Am I

That Know and

Still BE.

His mercy and kindness endure forever. His grace abounds for those who Love Him. Blessed are those who trust in the Lord. Live each day expecting a miracle!

# CHAPTER 8

# Christmas Joy

Christmas is my favorite day of the year and not because of the gifts we get to give or receive but the joy of the Savior being born to a virgin, teenage, Jewish girl named Mary (Luke 1:27). She said, "Yes" to the Angel Gabriel, who came to tell her she would have a child whose name will be Jesus, who is the Son of God (Luke 1:31–32). She said, "...Be it unto me according to thy word" (Luke 1:38 KJV).

I probably could have thought of at least a dozen other things to say, such as "I'm a virgin, remember?" or "No, I'm not ready to have a baby." "I'm only just engaged to Joseph, or I'm too young." And "What will Joseph think? What will people say?" But... She didn't. She concedes to God's will, and nine months later, she finds herself with Joseph on a donkey, traveling to Bethlehem, where she gives birth to Jesus in a cave or stable because there was no room left in the inn (Luke 2:4–5, 7). Different scholars believe it may have been a cave used as a stable. In any event, the angels did appear to the shepherds and told them to go see the child wrapped in swaddling clothes lying in a manger (Luke 2:12). The Magi followed the shining star in the East as Gentiles bearing gifts (Matthew 2:11).

I heard a joke that said if the Magi were three wise women instead of three wise men, it would have been a whole different story. They would have asked directions, got there on time, cleaned up the stable beforehand, helped with the delivery, and then made Mary and Joseph something to eat.[89] They would have been worth their weight in gold.

---

89 "If the Magi Were Women..." 2020. Beliefnet. 2020. https://www.beliefnet.com/entertainment/videojokes/jokes/christian/i/if-the-magi-were-women.aspx.

Christmas brings me such joy, the Christmas lights, Macy's windows, Santas in every mall, the boxes, the wrapping paper, the bows, the reindeer, camels, sheep, the little drummer boy, the infant Jesus and the Star, the Brightest Star and the Angels who sang. "Glory to God in the highest and peace to His people on Earth" (Luke 2:13–14). It's undeniable that Christmas is the best holiday, and that's not counting any gifts you may receive. The Christmas tree, the moonlight that shimmers off the snow covering the earth, the glimmer of the lights, the makings of snow angels and snowmen in the sunlight. I love Christmas. Keep Christ in Christmas. How could you not? It's all about pure love and giving. And that's Jesus. God is love... Emmanuel... God with us. And all the world is at peace, if not just for a moment, an hour, a day, a season. We should choose joy all year long, not just at Christmas. It is pure joy. Sure, it is a lot of work, don't get me wrong, but it's all joyful work.

The Christmas I had in 2013 at my house was a special Christmas. It was the first Christmas at my house since my divorce. I had obtained the home care job, so I could afford to host Christmas this year for my family. I have a big family (five siblings, spouses, and children). It was a white Christmas (even though the weatherman said we'd better pray for a miracle) with the snow sparkling against the lights. We bought a real blue spruce fir tree, and I decorated it with blue and silver decorations while my sons put up the Christmas lights. I had blue and white stars around the deck outside and little Christmas trees lining the walkway. Everyone received a little something from me; the nephews received mugs with candy, the nieces received plastic angels that lit up and sparkled iridescent colors when turned on. The adults received religious cutting boards with inspirational messages about love and family. I had the money to have the food catered, so all had plenty to eat with leftovers to take home.

Mom got many gifts, and unbeknownst to me, Mom had gotten gifts for all her six children, grandchildren, and spouses. I gave my Christmas prayer before dinner:

*Thank you, Lord, for sending your Son Jesus into Bethlehem on that Christmas morning. May we continue to be that Light in the world, spreading Love, Peace, and Hope into this world. Thank you Lord, for the many blessings you have bestowed upon us and continue to bless us with.*
*Amen.*

The best part was when my six-year-old niece opens the angel and says with enthusiasm and surprise, "This is soooo beautiful!" That made my day and the fact that my Christmas cactus bloomed for the first time in five years!

Christmas of 2014, I wrote:

*Jesus is the Reason for the Season*

*This Christmas, may you stop in wonder of each beautiful yet unique snowflake...*

*Jump in the snow and make that snow angel, no matter how old you are!*

*Bake that special batch of cookies from your favorite family recipe.*

*Give to that struggling family anonymously.*

*Take the time to listen to another's cares and woes.*

*Wrap that hard to find gift lovingly and beautifully.*

*Pray for someone you don't even like.*

*Offer encouragement and hope to the hopeless.*

*Shine His Light into the darkness.*

*Thank the Lord for everything you have.*

*Share His Peace and Joy in this world.*

*Find your heart and soul and give it to Jesus...*

*It's all He's ever wanted, anyway.*

Some of you may think, "OH Christmas. I have to have the family over again!" You think your family has drama. I know a family whose king fell in love with a married woman. Then he had her husband killed (Story of King David). One family got rid of their brother over the jealousy of a coat (Story of Joseph). They sold him into slavery. One woman had her husband sleep with the servant; (Story of Abraham). Every family has drama.

I love Christmas stories such as Scrooge being the meanest stingiest man and wound up being a good man.[90] Rudolph, the red-nosed reindeer, saw himself as a loser with an impediment, but he wound up being the star of the show that wintery, snowy day.[91] Ralph Kramden sells his prized possession, his bowling ball, to get his wife a gift for Christmas, only to find out she got him a bowling bag.[92] Linus in Charlie Brown's Christmas show always has his security blanket with him, but he doesn't need it when he reads from the Bible about the birth of Jesus.[93] The angels said to the shepherds. "Do not be afraid..." (Luke 2:10 NIV). That's how the love of God works, I suppose.

Christmas 2015, my motto was: *Just Believe.*

I made my own Christmas cards that year with the wise men on their camels following the star over Bethlehem with the words: BELIEVE written down the side of the page.

---

90 Scrooge, Ebeneezer, is the protagonist of Charles Dickens' 1943 novel "A Christmas Carol".
91 *Rudolph the Red Nosed Reindeer*—1964 fictional character in the Christmas animated TV special.
92 Ralph Kramer—*The Honeymooners*, played by Jackie Gleason in the 1950s.
93 Linus Van Pelt—is a fictional character in Charles M. Shultz's comic strip "Peanuts".

*B = brightest star in all of Bethlehem.*
*E = east from whence the wisemen came.*
*L = loved us so much He sent his only Son.*
*I = in a manger He lay.*
*E = ever to forgive us our sins.*
*V = virgin birth to Mary by the Holy Spirit*
*E = even the angels pronounce "Glory to God in*
*the Highest and Peace to his People on Earth."*

One night, I was thinking about the story of Christmas and about the innkeeper who said that "No, we don't have any room for you here" (Luke 2:7). There was a children's play about the birth of Christ and the little boy who played the innkeeper. After many practices, he knew his part. But on the day of the play, he instead says, "Yes, come in" because he could not bear to say "no" to baby Jesus. How many times have we closed the door on Jesus? How many times have we turned away and said "NO" to Him, "we're doing it our away, we don't need you"? How badly the innkeeper must have felt when he realized his mistake as a multitude of angels and the star, which shone so brightly over Bethlehem when heaven touched down to earth (Luke 2:13). And the innkeeper missed it...

Sometimes, we are like the innkeeper; we miss the big picture. There are so many "what ifs". What if only he had said, "Yes, we will make some room for you," to

Joseph and pregnant Mary. Maybe he (the innkeeper) and Joseph could have smoked a cigar outside celebrating the birth of his son, and maybe they could have become good friends. Mary could have had the innkeeper's wife help her with the birth, and she could have laid in a comfortable bed rather than straw. The star and the angels could have been shining and singing over the innkeeper's home, and he may have even been given a name and could have been the most famous innkeeper of all times. Gosh, he could have possibly had it all by just saying, "yes".

It makes me wonder how differently my life or yours could have turned out if we'd only said "yes" instead of the many times we've said "no" to the Lord. We need to be like that child in the play again and open our hearts to Jesus and say, "Yes, come inside Lord and stay and make this your home." We need to not only remember "Jesus is the reason for the season" and to "Keep Christ in Christmas," but to remember that "God so loved the world that he gave His only begotten Son" to redeem us (John 3:16 KJV). We need to know that love, joy, and peace that went into that first Christmas, and that is given to us every Christmas thereafter.

Christmas, no big deal, Bah Humbug, you say? Trust me. It is a big deal. If Mary had not said "Yes," you would all be going to HELL literally. Jesus came to us sent by God to shed his blood, die for us so that we could be saved (John 1:29). He was the ultimate sacrifice. He who was sinless paid the price for our sins in full (2 Corinthians 5:21). That's past, present, and future. NO, not a prophet, but only can the Son of God do that.

Most people say that Easter is the most important day in Christianity. Because that's the day Jesus rose from the dead after three days and after visiting people on earth, He then ascended into heaven (John 20:19; Acts1:9). Thus, promising us that death is not the end but just the beginning (Acts 1:11). But I think that Christmas is more important because if He was never born then He could never have died.

So... maybe Jesus wasn't born exactly on December 25. But He was born, and Mary, His mother, believed. She knew that the same God that gave Abraham's ninety-year-old wife Sarah, a child, could give herself, a virgin, one also (Genesis 18:17)—For nothing is impossible for our God. She didn't think about the ramifications; she truly lived outside the box.

Could you imagine what our friends and family would say if we told them God impregnated us? How absurd and ridiculous this sounds even today, nonetheless over 2,000 years ago? When God asked Abraham to sacrifice his only son to him on the altar after waiting over 100 years to have... until an angel stopped the knife before it bore down into to Isaac (Genesis 22:11–12). God had another plan. He sacrificed His only Son for us so that we could be redeemable to Him and have a relationship with Him again like the one Adam had before Satan interfered and ruined it. How about walking with God in the sunlight in a garden full of fresh fruits and vegetables, flowers, and wildlife (Genesis 3:8)? We can when Jesus comes again and makes a new heaven on earth (Revelation 21:1). It will be breathless, glorious, full of joy and contentment, void of all sickness, pain, and suffering (Revelation 21:4).

I've learned: Without love, there is no peace; without faith, there is no Hope, and Without hope, there is no Joy.

Choose joy. Choose love. Choose life. Choose Jesus. Choose to *Live Outside the Box* as these people did:

- It was grateful joy when Daniel was thrown into the lion's den and prayed to God, and the lion's mouths were shut closed, and they did not eat him (Daniel 6:22).
- It was a historical joy when Moses parted the Red Sea, and all the Israelites passed through safely, and when the Egyptians chased after them, the Red Sea swallowed them up (Exodus 14:16).
- It was a faith-filled joy for the woman who touched the hem of Jesus' gown and was instantly healed of twelve years of hemorrhaging (Luke 9:43–44).

- It was a life-saving joy for the woman caught in adultery from being stoned to death when he bent down and wrote on the ground with his finger and said, "Let the one among you who is without sin be the first to throw a stone at her" (John 8:7–8 EHV).
- It was a miraculous joy for the paralyzed man of thirty years lying by the pool of Bethesada to take up his mat and walk at Jesus' command (John 5:5–8).
- It was unexpected joy when Mary Magdalene went to the tomb on the third day and found the rock had been rolled away (John 20:1). And it was heartfelt joy when she heard Jesus say, "Mary" (John 20:16).
- And it was believing joy in the upper room for the apostle Thomas who saw Jesus' wounds on his hands, feet, and side (John 20:27–28).
- It was a redemptive joy when Peter jumps into the water when John says from the boat, "It is the Lord" standing on the shore (John 21:7). And when Jesus asked Peter 3 times if he loved Him and Peter answered "yes" 3 times (John 21:17).

Today...

It is the resounding joy of hearing your newborn baby's first cry.

It's the healing joy when the doctor says, "You're cancer free".

It's the relieved joy when after a disaster hits and you've lost everything that you had, and you learn your child is found still alive under all the rubble.

It's the comforting joy of knowing Jesus Loves You.

It's the everlasting joy of knowing there is a God, and there is a heaven to go to when you die.

The Joy of the Lord is my strength.

It is within our power to choose joy. DO NOT let anyone, including Satan, steal your joy.

There's a song called *Joy* by For King and Country which states, "I choose joy."[94] And *Smile* by the Sidewalk prophets who sing "There's always a reason to always choose Joy."[95]

Circumstances can try to steal our joy. Like the bedbugs on Christmas day and my family who didn't want me at their house (and rightfully so). I went to a restaurant with my good friend Amber and my kids instead. Or the torn ligament in my ankle two days before I was to get on a plane and travel to Chicago to see my son, which just meant with a wheelchair escort. Or the mean word from your boss telling you that a patient said

---

94 "Lyrics for Joy by For King & Country, 2018." 2020. Song Facts. 2020. https://www.songfacts.com/lyrics/for-king-country/joy.
95 "Sidewalk Prophets - Smile Lyrics, 2019." 2020. Azlyrics.Com. 2020. https://www.azlyrics.com/lyrics/sidewalkprophets/smile. html.

you look dirty and disheveled, while you were working through your own pain (which I knew just wasn't true). Or the co-worker who tries to sabotage your job and steal your joy by slandering your name and falsely accusing you of things you didn't do. Eventually, the truth came out, and that person was relieved of their position. Remember blessed are they who are persecuted for righteousness sake for theirs is the kingdom of heaven (Matthew 5:10 KJ21).

Because God is... Everything to everyone. He is Omnificent, omnipotent, and omnipresent. I wrote in my journal:

*He knows every thought you've ever thought,*
*Every dream you've ever sought,*
*He sees your every tear,*
*He feels your every fear,*
*He loves you more than*
*You could ever know,*
*Because He's paid the price for us to go*
*Redeemed to heaven*
*In Jesus' name,*
*Amen.*

Joy is not getting everything you want. It's about appreciating and feeling thankful for what you already have. I was wearing my "Today I Choose Joy" shirt on our way back from Europe with my sons when I needed double hip replacement surgery and was kind of doing a John Wayne swagger (as my physical therapist called it). Suddenly, a lady was pushing a wheelchair patient passed us, and she said, "You come with me,"

"But, I'm with them," I said.

She said, "Bring them too."

And she led us to the front of the line, and she said, "You shouldn't be waiting in that line in the condition you're in."

I was like "Really? OK, Thank you."

Unexpected joy came to me when I had the opportunity to go to the Holy Land with Father. R. and my friend Loretta. I had just told my Bible group that I would love to go to the Holy Land to walk where Jesus walked. Then, as I went to the shrine of Our Lady, I saw a flyer that Father R. was taking people to the Holy Land! I was ecstatic! I called my friend Loretta to see if she would go with me. I figured if she said "Yes," then it was within God's will. She said, "Yes!" It was a beautiful trip just knowing I was there where He was. We went to see where he was born in Bethlehem. Down fourteen steps into the cave, and we saw the manger where Jesus was placed into. It was surreal to go to the Holy Sepulcher church to see where Jesus was crucified and died. It was a memorable joy when Fr. R. asked the men to play *How Great Thou Art* and instead, the men on the boat played *How Great Is Our God* by Chris Tomlin. We got to sing *How Great Is Our God* on a boat on the Sea of Galilee. It is a joyous memory that I will never forget. Look up Chris Tomlin's World Edition on YouTube. It's well worth the look.

Joy is knowing you did your best for your patients and thanking God for the courage and wisdom given to you. Joy is avoiding the near accident, and knowing your angels played a part in that. Joy is giving hope to others. Joy is knowing you make a difference. Joy is knowing You matter. The Joy of the Lord is my strength (Nehemiah 8:10 NKJV). I didn't think I was going to be able to serve twenty-one people on Christmas 2018 due to my hobbling around. The decorating, cleaning, and preparing all of the food and drinks. But with God's help and my sons', we pulled it off together. It was good.

Joy is knowing you have friends that will stick with you through thick and thin. Joy is knowing your children are safe and that you would do anything for them. Joy is knowing you have done everything in your power for them. Joy is knowing that you have family and that you have done all you can to help them as they have for you. Joy is knowing they all love you just the way you are. Joy is inner peace. The kind of peace Jesus gives, not as the world gives. Joy is knowing you are loved by the Almighty God, and He has a plan for your life. You're not here by mistake or by atoms crashing into one another. There is a rhyme and reason to it all. There is a purpose for everything under the heavens—Which brings me to Hope. "Faith is the substance of things hoped for; the evidence of things not seen" (Hebrews 11:1 NKJV). In other words, faith is being sure of what we hope for and certain of what we do not see. Or as Carl Sagan, the late and noted agnostic, astrophysicist, philosopher, and author once said, "Absence of evidence is not evidence of absence."[96] This means just because you don't have proof something exists does not mean it doesn't exist. As Danny Gokey sings in his song, *Just Haven't Seen It Yet.*

To have hope is to trust; to trust is to have hope. We hope and pray and trust that God will make everything alright.

We all hope to some degree. We hope our car will start on a frigid morning, so we can get to work. Or we hope we get the job, we hope our loved one survives the operation, we hope it doesn't rain, or we hope they will like the gift; we hope for all sorts of things before they happen.

Sometimes hope looks like a dream God has placed on your heart.

---

96 "Carl Sagan." n.d. *Wikipedia, The Free Encyclopedia.* 2020. https://en.wikipedia.org/wiki/Carl_Sagan.

The Wright brothers hoped their invention of an airplane would fly.[97]

Thomas Edison hoped his light bulb would become a commodity for everyday usage.[98]

Henry Ford hoped his automobile would one day be the mode of transportation for most people rather than horse and buggy.[99]

Without hope, there could be nothing to dream about. Without Hope, the cancer patient wouldn't entertain the thought of having chemotherapy and radiation. Without hope, we would not anticipate a brighter future or the birth of our baby. Without hope, we would all be depressed with nothing to look forward to. Without any hope, we could not go through the difficulties of this world and know we will recover and see the light again. So many people suffer from hopelessness and

97 Wright Brothers—"Orville and Wilbur were two American Aviaion pioneersgenerally credited with inventing, building, and flying the world's first successful motor operated airplane (…) December 17, 1903" ("Wright Brothers." 2020. *Wikipedia, The Free Encyclopedia*. 2020. https://en.wikipedia.org/wiki/Wright_brothers).
98 Thomas Edison—Thomas Alva Edison, "American inventor and businessman who has been described as America's greatest inventor." He invented the telegraph, phonograph, incandescent light bulb in 1879 ("Thomas Edison." 2020. *Wikipedia, The Free Encyclopedia*. 2020. https://en.wikipedia.org/wiki/Thomas_Edison).
99 Henry Ford— "American industrialist and business magnate, founder of Ford Motor Company" and created the Model T in 1908, and went on to develop the assemblyline mode of production which revolutionized the automobile industry selling millions of cars ("Henry Ford." 2020. *Wikipedia, The Free Encyclopedia*. 2020. https://en.wikipedia.org/wiki/Henry_Ford).

depression. Suicide is a form of hopelessness. A kind word or a smile can go a long way—Practice kindness... Live compassion.

Martin Luther King Jr. was quoted to saying, "We must accept finite disappointment but never lose infinite hope."[100][101] Franklin D. Roosevelt once said, "We have always held to the hope, the belief, the conviction that there is a better life a better world, beyond the horizon."[102][103]

Sitting in the upper room with the apostles, the blessed mother of Jesus, Mary, could have given up her faith and hope of ever seeing her son again after watching her only Son tortured and hung on a cross (Acts 1:14). But she believed and trusted that God would have a good ending to the story. And He did. She must have hoped against all hope that her Son would rise up from the grave like He said He would. Her unimaginable

---

100 "Quote by Martin Luther King Jr." 2020. Goodreads, Inc. 2020. https://www.goodreads.com/quotes/37292-we-must-accept-finite-disappointment-but-never-lose-infinite-hope.
101 Martin Luther King Jr.— "was an American Christian minister and activist who became the most visible spokesperson and leader in the civil rights movement from 1955 until his assassination in 1968" "Martin Luther King Jr." (2020. *Wikipedia, The Free Encyclopedia*. 2020. https://en.wikipedia.org/wiki/Martin_Luther_King_Jr.).
102 "Quote by Franklin Delano Roosevelt." 2020. Goodreads, Inc. 2020. https://www.goodreads.com/quotes/1017824-we-have-always-held-to-the-hope-the-belief-the.
103 "Franklin D. Roosevelt." 2020. *Wikipedia, The Free Encyclopedia*. 2020. https://en.wikipedia.org/wiki/Franklin_D._Roosevelt.

joy came in the upper room when she heard Jesus say, "Mom" or probably, "Mother" as He embraced her.

*May the God of hope fill you with all joy and peace as you trust in Him, so that you may overflow with hope by the power of the Holy Spirit.*

(Romans 15:13 NIV)

It's a lot like Faith.

*Faith is to believe what you do not see the reward of this faith is to see what you believe.*

—St. Augustine[104]

We have faith that we will awaken in the morning. We have faith that the chair we sit on will not collapse from our weight. We have faith that our candidate for office is the right one for the job. We have faith that our children will be safe at school. We have faith that we will get our paycheck at the end of the week. We have faith in the surgeon that does our operation. We have faith in our soldiers fighting for our freedom. We should have the faith of our forefathers, One Nation Under God.

---

104 "Quote by Saint Augustine." 2020. Goodreads, Inc. 2020. https://www.goodreads.com/quotes/32262-faith-is-to-believe-what-you-do-not-yet-see.

Noah had faith and built an ark for a flood he had never seen of nor heard of (Genesis 6:14, 17). Imagine his neighbors weren't too happy with that monstrosity on his front lawn and the heckling!

David had enough faith that His God would able him to kill a giant with just a stone and a slingshot (1 Samuel 17:50). I'm sure all bets were off that day!

When Moses parted the Red Sea, he must have had enormous faith to step into that water with his staff, and I'm sure he hoped he wasn't going to look like a fool and have his entire nation annihilated by Pharaoh's army (Exodus 14:27).

Or Joshua, after seven days of circling the city of Jericho. I'm sure he was hoping the Lord would bring down the walls of the city, and he had enough faith to win the victory that day (Joshua 6:15).

I'm sure Elijah was hoping that God was going to light his altar after dousing it with water three times, in front of the 450 pagan priests who were literally going to roast him alive if God didn't set it ablaze (1 Kings 18:38).

Gideon, with only 300 men against 135,000 enemies, was hoping that God was going to fight this battle for him since it seemed like impossible odds (Judges 7:6).

The apostles were hoping against all hope that Jesus would rise from the dead after three days and that He was who He said He was (Luke 24:6, 7).

On August 22, 2017 I wrote:

> *Lord,*
> *Give me the Faith of just a mustard seed*
> *To move mountains,*
> *Give me the power to*
> *Heal the sick,*
> *Give me the Love to*
> *Feed the poor,*
> *Lord, give me the Strength to*
> *House the orphans and widows,*
> *Give me the wisdom to*
> *Proclaim the gospel to*
> *All nations and Lord give me your*
> *Peace that surpasses All understanding to*
> *Do the will of God through the Holy Spirit*
> *In the name of Jesus Christ.*
> *Amen.*

Jesus himself said, "Everything is possible for one who has faith" (Mark 9:23 NABRE). Or "If you can believe, all things are possible to him who believes" (Mark 9:23 NKJV).

Christine Caine and her husband had enough faith to live outside the box with God. They started an anti-sex trafficking organization.[105] She was told it could NOT be done. She stepped out of her boat onto uncharted waters with faith and found unexpected miracles. God stepped in when she could not do it by herself. He shows up and shows off. She now has a worldwide organization saving young children and women from sex traffickers. She believed and knew that with God, all things are possible. She sees God intervening all the time.

During my *Gideon* Bible study by Priscilla Shirer, I heard her talking about when Christine was in a country that didn't have the funds to police the brothel where young girls were being kept against their will. So they and others prayed. They did not pray for money but for God to change the hearts of the men going in to be serviced by these young girls. She saw God change the heart of one man who changed his mind when he went into the brothel. When he learned that the girl was there against her will, he brought the girl to the police station. It all starts with just one person to make a difference.

---

105 Christine Caine— "is an Australian activist, evangelist, author, and international speaker. Caine and her husband Nick are best known for founding The A21 Campaign in 2008, a 501(c)(3) non-profit, non-governmental organization that combats human trafficking" ("Christine Caine." 2020. *Wikipedia, The Free Encyclopedia.* 2020. https://en.wikipedia.org/wiki/Christine_Caine.).

I remember an African American woman with stage IV breast cancer, which had spread to her bones. She was in a lot of pain and taking pain killers. We talked, and she happened to be an LPN, and she also worked in a state hospital as I once did for psychiatric patients. I told her I went back to school and got my RN. She had married and had children and took in foster children, some of whom I had the pleasure of meeting. They were grown and were bringing their mother some of her favorite foods because they knew she wasn't eating very much these days. I asked her if she had faith, and she said yes and that she was hoping to go to heaven.

It's peculiar how people who are close to death know it. She told me she did not want to die at home because she did not want her grandchildren, who were very young, five and ten years old, to remember her that way. It was now nearing Christmas, and she had the Christmas tree all lit up with life-sized black angel dolls, which I commented on. I told her how I'd never seen such beautiful angel dolls before. Somehow, she knew this would be her last Christmas. She was now on heavy pain killers, and she met with me, but she was asleep when I arrived. She told me that she did not want her grandchildren to find her dead in her bed. I told her to have faith and that I would pray for her. I wished her a blessed Christmas, and I would catch up with her around New Years. When I called to see her, her hus-

band said, "She passed away in the hospital last night."
I said, "Oh, I'm very sorry for your loss." As I hung up
the phone, a tear fell as I thought how merciful God was
as He gave her the grace to die with dignity in a hospital
and not in front of her grandchildren.

"Faith is the power of love and God, which produces
hope and brings us joy," I've heard it said.

Have HOPE, Seek JOY, Live FAITH, and LOVE one
another.

LAURA RIVIEZZO-TAGGART

# CHAPTER 9

# Love One Another

The priest played the song *All You Need is Love* by The Beatles for his first day as a pastor. In light of love, wouldn't loving one another be a new concept in this world? No. Jesus said, "...Love one another as I have loved you" (John 15:12 NKJV). That means you, me, the Jew, the Muslim, the Hindu, the Buddhist, the Christian, the rich, the poor, the straight, the gay, the good, the bad, and the ugly, so to speak.

Stop.

Imagine a world with no wars, no segregation, no biases, no shootings of innocent children and people, no bullying, no judging, no hatred, no homelessness, no keeping up with the Jones's. Just a world where all are equal, all are treated with respect and dignity. Competition would be done fairly based on qualifications, not on who you know or are related to with the same with the opportunities to move up the corporate ladder. There would be no black lives matter or blue blood matters. If we truly loved one another, it wouldn't matter if one is white, black, Hispanic, Asian, Indian, Jew, Greek, or Gentile. It wouldn't matter who you are. We could all live in peace.

Like on that day in Bethlehem when love came down from heaven when Mary wrapped Him in swaddling clothes and laid Him in a manger (Luke 2:7). We are all created by the same God who created the heavens and the earth and blew breath into the dirt, and made man (Genesis 2:7). If we could just love one another, the way Jesus showed us, the fulfillment of the ten commandments would be made easy.

*You will have no other gods before me. You will not worship or make any false idols. You will keep holy the Sabbath day, honor your mother and father, and never lie steal, covet, commit adultery, murder or take the Lord God's name in vain.*

(Exodus 20:1–17 NIV)

Sounds easy right? Not really, we are not there yet, not even close, even after over 2,000 years!

But... you can make a difference and be that voice crying out in the desert "Repent (...) prepare ye the way of the Lord" (Matthew 3:2–3 KJV) —For He is coming. Be the light that overcomes the darkness, stand for truth, do the right thing even when you think no one else is looking. Give to the poor, feed the hungry, if it means helping to end slave trafficking, or the drug/alcohol addicted, homeless, or prostitute and help them to get their lives back on track. Help the teenager struggling with her baby because she chose to have her child over abortion, volunteer at a soup kitchen, help people that have been hit by an earthquake, flood, or other natural disasters.

If none of these resources are within your reach, pray, and then pray some more. St. Paul said, "Pray without ceasing" (1 Thessalonians 5:17). Why? Because prayer is powerful. Prayer took the chains off of St. Peter's arms and legs while in a prison cell in Rome, and he walked right past the guards and out of prison with the help of God's two angels because his people were praying for him (Acts 12:7–9).

I learned from Matthew Kelly, who wrote *Rediscover Jesus* that "Jesus was a radical."[106] It was radical teaching to preach "love your enemies" and "to forgive seventy times seven times" and "turn the other cheek" (Luke 6:27; Matthew 18:22, 5:39 NKJV). And to "love one another as I have loved you" and "love your neighbor as yourself," pretty radical stuff, huh? Even more so, to the Jewish priests of that time (John 15:12; Luke 10:27).

Jesus came to show us the way; we need to follow in his footsteps. Sure, I'd love to cure people of cancer, give sight to the blind, hearing to the deaf, speech to the mute, and casting out demons (Matthew 15:31; Luke 4:33, 35). But most of us aren't there yet. Jesus said, "If you have faith of a mustard seed you can move mountains, nothing would be impossible for you (Matthew 17:20). I know I can't move mountains yet; what does that say about the size of my faith? Thankfully, Jesus said, "I will pray the Father, and He will give you another Helper, that He may abide with you forever" (John 14:16 NKJV). His other names are, Advocate, Counselor, Paraclete, Comforter, Holy Spirit.

I know the Holy Spirit moves in me, and there are times I feel Him, and tears just start to fall down my face. I'm not accustomed to speaking in tongues, like my friend Renuka, but we all have been given different gifts from the Holy Spirit, and I don't think that was

---

106  Kelly. 2015.

one of mine. They say He collects every tear (Psalm 56:8); well, I'm sure he has a big vat full of mine!

My grandmother used to cry when she was happy or sad, and I never understood it. I'd say, "Grandma, why are you crying?" Tears of joy in good times and tears of sadness in dark times. Now, I understand it because I do it. My grandmother was like a mom to me. I stayed with her as a child while my parents worked. I know I have my mother to thank for convincing my father to let me stay with her again as a teenager, so I could finish nursing school. They were moving to North Carolina. I was her first grandchild, and do I dare say her favorite? I remember that she taught me to pray to St. Dymphna.[107] She treated me like I was the only one who mattered. It's the closest thing I have that can equate to God's love for me.

I'd always say, "God loves you or smile, Jesus loves you, on a smiley face." For years I'd say this to my kids. And I would believe it because there's the song that goes, "Jesus loves me this I know for the Bible tells me so."[108] But... I could not feel it. I knew it intellectually but physically or emotionally, no. I was always the doer; I was taking care of everyone else's needs, physically,

---

107 "Dymphna." 202AD. *Wikipedia, The Free Encyclopedia*. 202AD. https://en.wikipedia.org/wiki/Dymphna.
108 "Jesus Loves Me, This I Know by Anna Bartlett Warner." 2020. Hymnary.Org. 2020. https://hymnary.org/text/jesus_loves_me_this_i_know_for_the_bible.

emotionally, spiritually—then I didn't have time for my own.

One day someone said to me at Bible study, "God loves YOU very much." I just made a joke, but then when I went home, I pondered it, and I started to see it as well as feel it. The moment of truth came in the movie The Shack adapted by William Paul Young's novel. When Mack says, "You abandoned Him, just like you abandoned me."[109] Papa (plays God the Father) says, "I've never left you, and I love You so much."[110] Well, that opened the floodgates of tears right in the movie theater. It was then, I realized that God really does love me, with all my flaws and weaknesses, with all the sinful things that I've done in my lifetime. I'll admit there were times I'd felt abandoned, and times where I've questioned His mere existence. I'd say, "Where are you, God?" Or "Where were you when... ?"

My sister Christine said to my youngest sister, "She feels things 100 percent more than the average person does." Well, I don't know if that's a blessing or a curse, but all I do know now without a doubt is that God loves me. He's brought me this far. Through a divorce, a mental breakdown, a home to provide for my boys, money to pay the bills, a retirement pension, a job after retire-

109 "The Shack Movie, Based on the Novel by William Paul Young." n.d. Lionsgate.Com. 2020. https://www.lionsgate.com/movies/the-shack.
110 Ibid.

ment, surviving bedbugs, the leasing of a new car, the quitting of a job, two total hip replacement surgeries, sprained ankle with torn ligaments and the writing of HIS book. And it's been said that His latter days will be better than His former days (Job 8:7). I can't wait to see what He yet has in store for me!

I love the Lord with all my heart and soul. If it's too hard or painful, I lay it down at the cross and ask Him to help me carry it, and He does. That's love. For all you Mom's out there, how much do you love your children? Okay, times that by 7.8 billion (the number of people in the world today) that's how much God loves us because first and foremost, we are All his children.[111]

One of the hardest things I've had to do in my life is to put my half shepherd—half chow, thirteen-year-old dog, Simon, to sleep. As I held him and I pet his head and tearfully said, "Mommy loves you, and Jesus loves you too." As I thought about it and him, I was reminded of how a dog loves his master unconditionally. Boy, how we could learn from this simple creature, to love our Lord, our Master:

A dog trusts his master to feed him every day.

His health is in the hands of the master.

He trusts that his Master will come home and care for him.

---

111 "World Population Clock: 7.8 Billion People (2020)." 2020. Worldometers.Info. 2020. https://www.worldometers.info/world-population/.

A dog is faithful to his master and will serve his master all the days of his life.

A dog doesn't ask for anything in return but to be loved.

And isn't that just what we all want?

There's a song *Fighting for Me* by Riley Clemmons that is phenomenal. Once you realize that God loves you, fights for you, and is always there for you when there is no one else or when you've got nothing else, you know it will be ok and that you can pour out His love onto others. He's "The God Who Stays," as Matthew West sings.[112]

St. Josephine Bakhita was born in Sudan in 1869.[113] At the age of seven, she was kidnapped and sold into slavery. She was brutally beaten and tortured until she came into Italy and was declared a free person, and she was then baptized. She said, "I am indeed loved." And it all started because she wanted to know who the maker of the moon and the stars were. She was canonized a saint in 2000 by Pope John Paul ll.[114]

---

112 "Behind The Song: Matthew West Shares The Story Behind The Song 'The God Who Stays.'" 2019. Freeccm.Com. 2020. https://freeccm.com/2019/10/29/behind-the-song-matthew-west-shares-the-story-behind-the-song-the-god-who-stays/.
113 Josephine Margaret Bakhita— "a Sudanese-Italian Canossan religious sister born a slave in Sudan in 1869" ("Josephine Bakhita." 2020. *Wikipedia, The Free Encyclopedia.* 2020. https://en.wikipedia.org/wiki/Josephine_Bakhita.).
114 Ibid.

God's love is unconditional. Nothing you could say or do would make God love you any more or any less. Jesus died for us sinners; he ate with Zacchaeus, a tax collector and sinner (Luke 19:2, 5). "...God so loved the world that He gave his Only Begotten Son" to die for our sins on a cross (John 3:16 NKJV). What can separate us from the Love of Christ? I think St. Paul knows.

He says, "...neither death nor life, nor angels, nor principalities not present things nor future things nor powers nor height nor depth nor any other creature will be able to separate us from the love of God in Christ Jesus Our Lord" (Romans 8:38 ?) and He should know. He was blinded, shipwrecked, bitten by a deadly snake, had a thorn in his side, imprisoned, whipped , and it is thought that he was beheaded (Acts 9:8, 27:43–44, 28:4–5; 2 Corinthians 12:7; Acts 28:17; 2 Corinthians 11:24).

Love wasn't proven by the miracles Jesus performed, but by His dying on the cross and rising again on the third day—Promising us hope for life after death. God's love is beyond all space and time as we understand it. You can't escape God's love for you just need to look at what happened to Jonah (Jonah 2:1). You can reject it, which is very saddening because God still loves you and is always waiting for you with open arms, just like the one lost sheep of the ninety-nine that He went back for (Matthew 18:13–14). Or... the prodigal son whose father welcomed him back with open arms and threw him a party (Luke 16:23–24)! St. Augustine said, "God loves each of us as if there were only one of us" (paraphrase).[115] God's love is immeasurable and incomprehensible. It doesn't fit in a box. You can truly live outside the box.

Love shatters loneliness; love makes the world go round, love matters, love conquers evil, love never fails. "Love conquers a multitude of sins," as St. Peter said (1 Peter 4:8 NASB). Love wins. Do everything out of Love—Love for God, creation, and one another. Let Love be sincere; hate what is evil hold onto what is good.

*Love is the beauty of the soul.*

—St. Augustine [116]

St. Paul said,

*If I speak in human and angelic tongues but do not have love I am a resounding gong or a clashing cymbal. And if I have the gift of prophecy and comprehend all mysteries and all knowledge; if I have all faith so as to move mountains but do not have Love I am nothing. If I give away everything I*

---

115 "Augustine Quote." 2019. Fauxtations Wordpress. 2019. https://fauxtations.wordpress.com/2019/08/29/augustine-god-loves-each-of-us/.
116 "Quote by Saint Augustine of Hippo." 2020. Goodreads, Inc. 2020. https://www.goodreads.com/quotes/24726-love-is-the-beauty-of-the-soul.

*own, and if I hand over my body over so that I may boast but do not have love, I gain nothing.*

(1 Corinthians 3:1–3 NABRE)

St. Paul told the Corinthians:

*Love is patient, love is kind. It is not jealous, is not pompous, it is not inflated, it is not rude, it does not seek its own interests, it is not quick-tempered, it does not brood over injury, it does not rejoice over wrongdoings, but rejoices in the truth. It bears all things, believes all things, hopes all things, endures all things.*

(1 Corinthians 13:4–6 NABRE)

*...Faith, hope, and love, but the greatest of these is Love.*

(1 Corinthians 13:13 NIV)

God knows you, God knew you, God has always known you since before you were born (Psalm 139:13).

God forgives you, God forgave you, God has already forgiven you because Jesus Christ, His Son, has paid for your sins in full (1 John 2:2).

God so loved the world that He sent His only begotten Son to redeem you, me, us (John 3:16).

Part of loving one another is sharing the gospel with others so they too may come to know and love Jesus. Evangelizing comes in many forms. It's not just standing up on the altar and preaching. Although this works for some, it may be in a book, song, a video, an online sermon, a podcast, radio, TV, a Bible group. For some, it's literally taking the Word into the world with their own hands and feet like Jesus and His apostles did, and missionaries around the world still do today.

St. Patrick was one of those "hands-on type of guys."[117] He was captured and sold into slavery to Ireland from ages sixteen to twenty-two. He had an angel tell him to get on a ship. He went to the shore, and there was a ship (probably a pirate or trader's ship). He prayed and convinced them to let him on. He went to Auxerre, France, and studied to be a priest. He then had a calling to return to Ireland (it was considered the ends of the earth as they knew it) to preach the gospel to them as Jesus had said.

Likewise Pope John Paul II was an amazing leader. He initiated World Youth Day and went to a different country each year to speak to the youth about the gos-

---

117 Saint Patrick— "Fifth century Romano-British Christian missionary and Bishop of Ireland. Known as "Apostle of Ireland," he is the primary patron saint of Ireland, (…) venerated in Catholic Church, Eastern Orthodox, Anglican and Lutheran." ("Saint Patrick." 2020. *Wikipedia, The Free Encyclopedia*. 2020. https://en.wikipedia.org/wiki/Saint_Patrick.).

pel and of faith.[118] While he was a Polish priest, who taught in universities during the Nazi regime, about love and hope and peace. He said Christmas eve mass for the polish workers as bishop of Krakow, Poland. He would take students kayaking and skiing. He was always centered around the young people. He knew the importance of making the next generation aware of Jesus's teachings, so it would be carried through and not forgotten about. Most of us are now senior citizens who are the product of that generation. We must find a way to get through to our children and our children's children, so they, too, will come to know Jesus Christ as their Lord and savior.

Another important leader was Billy Graham.[119] He also proclaimed the gospel to people of all ages. Many of us are now are the result of that great evangelist, the

---

118  Pope John Paul ll—born Karol Jozef Wojtyla in Wadowce,Poland,1920 he traveled to 129 countries in 104 trips outside of Italy. Head of Catholic church in 1978 until his death- April 2, 2005, surviving WW ll ,studying in clandestine classes and aiding Jews during the war; he was ordained a priest Nov. 1946 , taught as a professor at Catholic University of Lublin, became archbishop of Krakow, Poland Dec. 1963 by Pope Paul Vl ("Pope John Paul II." 2020. *Wikipedia, The Free Encyclopedia*. 2020. https://en.wikipedia. org/wiki/Pope_John_Paul_II.).
119  Billy Graham—Franklin Graham Jr. American evangelist, prominent evangelical Christian figure, an ordained Southern Baptist minister. One of his biographers has placed him "among the most influential Christian leaders" of the 20th century ("Billy Graham." 2020. *Wikipedia, The Free Encyclopedia*. 2020. https:// en.wikipedia.org/wiki/Billy_Graham.).

baby boomers. But most of us are not the "young, in crowd" any longer. But who will carry on to the younger generations?

I was contemplating this the other day when I was told that Kanye West has become a Christian and is now saved.[120] I thought, *Oh well, God can use anyone. He used Moses, didn't he?* Kanye released a new album called *Jesus is King*. He also has a following of younger adults, generation X, Z, and the millennials; if they can hear the Word of God from a rap star, then they too may think it is a good thing and start to believe. In today's world, it doesn't seem too outlandish to me. Hey, it's a start, anyway.

Pope Francis is now carrying out the tradition of World Youth Day in speaking to the younger generations in different countries around the world.[121] He speaks to hundreds of thousands of people. It is celebrated every two to three years with a large international gathering, and on the off years, there is a smaller celebration in Rome.

120 Kanye West—"Jesus Is King" album-released October 25,2019 through GOOD Music distributed by Def. Jam Recordings. ("Kanye West." 2020. *Wikipedia, The Free Encyclopedia*. 2020. https:// en.wikipedia.org/wiki/Kanye_West.).
121 Pope Francis—Born Jorge Mario Bergoglia on Dec. 1936 in Argentina; ordained a priest in 1969 is the first Jesuit pope, first pope from the Southern Hemisphere .He was elected pope in 2016 until present. ("Pope Francis." 2020. *Wikipedia, The Free Encyclopedia*. 2020. https://en.wikipedia.org/wiki/Pope_Francis.).

Steven Furtick, a thirty-nine-year-old pastor, song-writer, and New York Times best-selling author.[122] He is the founder and pastor of Elevation Worship Church's global ministry, and he appeals to a younger generation of people.

On November 7, I wrote:

> *Lord, don't just let me see-*
> *Give me a vision,*
> *Lord don't let me hear-*
> *Make me listen,*
> *Lord, don't give me a path,*
> *Give me the way,*
> *Lord, don't give me a melody,*
> *Give me a song to sing,*
> *Lord, don't give me a willingness,*
> *Give me faith,*
> *Lord don't give me worry*
> *Give me trust,*
> *Lord don't give me courage*
> *Without your wisdom,*
> *Lord, don't give me just promises,*

---

122 Steven Furtick—Born February 19,1980, Steven Furtick Jr. founder and pastor of multi-site global ministry of Elevation church through , online streaming television and music .He holds a Master of Divinity degree from Southern Baptist Theological Seminary and author of several books. ("Steven Furtick." 2020. *Wikipedia, The Free Encyclopedia.* 2020. https://en.wikipedia.org/ wiki/Steven_Furtick.).

*Give me hope*
*Lord, don't give me tranquility,*
*Without Your peace*
*Lord, don't give me just happiness,*
*Give me joy,*
*Lord, don't just give me compassion,*
*But give me your Love for my neighbor and*
*myself.*
*Amen.*

Jesus said, "NO greater Love has one then to lay down his life for his friends" (John 15:13 NABRE). Doesn't every soldier do that for their fellow soldiers? Doesn't every policeman, fireman, do that on a daily basis for strangers and their fellow officers? But could I take a bullet for a perfect stranger? I don't know. I know I'd take a bullet for my kids, parent, sibling, or even possibly a close friend. But I cannot honestly say if I would or would not for a complete stranger. But that is what St. Maximillian Kolbe did. Maximillian Kolbe was a Franciscan friar in Poland who gave up his life in the Auschwitz German death camp for a stranger.[123] Ten men

---

123 Maximilian Kolbe- Born Raymund Kolbe on January 8, 1894 to Aug.14 1941 was a Polish Conventual Franciscan friar in German occupied Poland; founder ; He was venerated a saint canonized October 10,1982 by Pope John Paul ll, venerated in Catholic, Lurtheran and Anglican churches ("Maximilian Kolbe." 2020. *Wikipedia, The Free Encyclopedia.* 2020. https://en.wikipedia.org/wiki/Maximilian_Kolbe.).

LIVING OUTSIDE THE BOX

were picked to die because of an escape. Fr. Kolbe voluntarily took the place of a man named Franciszek Gajowniczek, who had a family. He endured three weeks of intolerable suffering of starvation, and when only he and three other men were left, they were injected with carbonic acid. He died on August 14, 1941, and was canonized on October 12, 1982, by Pope John Paul II.[124]

So many Christians around the world are being persecuted for their faith. Thankfully, we in America are not. But what if you were told if you renounce Jesus, you could live, or you were to be beheaded? I pray that day never comes. But even more so, I pray that I would have the courage to stand firm in the faith as St. Paul did. Or, take it down a notch...

What if you're supposed to love someone, but you're finding it very difficult? They've hurt you or lied to you; well, that's where forgiveness comes into play. Life with my ex-husband, I'm supposed to love him because he is a child of God and father of my children. I find it very difficult to love him. I am trying to forgive him for all the pain he's caused myself and my sons.

Or to love your enemies? To love the person who murdered your loved one? To love the person who raped your son or daughter or you? To love the person who swindled your life savings with a phony scam? To love the person who abuses their wife or children? I don't

124 Ibid.

225

understand it all, but that's when I just pray for them and trust God. It's all any of us can do. Stand in Hope. He knows, He sees, He hears, and He knows the why. We can't, and we don't.

Agape love—Loving without reservation. Loving for the sake of love. Loving unconditionally. Loving all because they are all children of God. Loving even if it's difficult. Loving not for what will be our reward. Loving when all the world is hating. Loving in all situations. Unimaginable, unending, unrelenting love that is the love in which Jesus has for us.

Love is a noun but when applied it is really a verb. As Mother Teresa said, "Intense love does not measure. It just gives."[125] [126] God is love. God loves you today, tomorrow, and yesterday. He never changes. Love determines our way in this life. You can choose love, or you can choose hate. Love is from God; the other is not. So, never think that you are incapable of being loved. Here are some of the least who was still loved by Jesus.

125 "Quote by Mother Teresa." 2020. Goodreads, Inc. 2020. https://www.goodreads.com/quotes/153541-intense-love-does-not-measure-it-just-gives.

126 Mother Theresa- Saint Theresa of Calcutta was an Albanian-Indian Roman Catholic nun and missionary .Founder of the Order of the Missionaries of Charity which expanded to 610 foundations in 123 countries. Born Aug.26,1910 in Skopje, North Macedonia and died in Kolkata India on Sept. 5,1997. She was canonized a saint by Pope Francis on Sept. 4, 2016.Won the 1979 Nobel Peace Prize. ("Mother Teresa." 2020. *Wikipedia, The Free Encyclopedia.* 2020. https://en.wikipedia.org/wiki/Mother_Teresa.).

- Jesus loved the Samaritan woman at the well who had been married five times before (John 4:9, 18).
- Jesus loved the prostitute caught in adultery, who was about to be stoned (John 8:3, 5, 11).
- Jesus loved the man possessed with a legion of demons (Mark 5:2, 9).
- Jesus loved the paralytic man they lowered down on a mat through the roof where He was speaking (Mark 2:4, 11).
- Jesus loved the ten lepers (Luke 17:12–14).
- Jesus loved the man blind from birth (John 9:1, 7).
- Jesus loved the Centurion's servant (Luke 7:2, 10).
- Jesus loved the tax collector, Zacchaeus (Luke 19:2, 5).
- Jesus loved his friend Lazarus (John 11:5, 44).
- Jesus loved Saul, who was persecuting the Christians (later St. Paul) (Acts 9:1, 18).

Jesus loves us. He died on a cross for us. Even when we were all still sinners. This is Agape Love.

"For God so loved the world that He gave His only Begotten Son for us" (John 3:16).—To redeem us.

To follow in Jesus' footsteps is to practice Agape Love. As Francis de Sales said, "The measure of Love is to Love without measure."[127] We must love until it over-flows from us onto others. We were made to love one another as He loved us. Big shoes to fill for sure. But no man is an island; we were made to be a family, a church, a community. Here are some examples of Jesus' love in the world today:

Jesus loved the little ninety-two-year-old German man whose wife had passed away. They had no children. He was drafted into Hitler's army. He and his wife came to live in America after the war. Now all he has left are the pictures of her hanging on the walls of their home and the memories of them together. He had been staying in bed for days in the middle of summer without any air conditioning, without eating or drinking anything, in an attempt to end his life. Unsuccessful at his attempt, he now had to learn to find the will to live without her.

Jesus loved the man diagnosed with Schizophrenia. His wife was very dedicated and made sure he took all his medications and attended all his doctor appointments. Their hobby was collecting 45rpm records for their jukebox.

Jesus loved the man diagnosed with Lou Gehrig's disease. He could not stand by himself nor dress him-

127 "Quote by Francis de Sales." 2020. Goodreads, Inc. 2020. https://www.goodreads.com/quotes/32909-the-measure-of-love-is-to-love-without-measure.

self. His wife told me he loved his man cave, where he drank his whiskey and smoked his cigars. He was advised against these two things but refused to give them up. He saw many doctors until the last doctor said, "I don't think you have Lou Gehrig's disease."

Jesus loved the woman who was depressed after finding her husband dead by strangulation in the basement in an apparent suicide.

Jesus loved the man with the double above the knee amputation from uncontrolled diabetes. He was in a wheelchair. He wheeled himself over to the door to let his two dogs go outside to play in the yard. A tear escaped his eyes as he probably realized he would never be able to walk them again.

Jesus loved the nun who had bipolar disorder. She is now in a nursing home. We would talk about her life as a teacher or about Pope Francis' visit to New York.

Jesus loved the eighty-something year-old-woman with brittle diabetes who was found unconscious by her son. Luckily, her son lived next door. She had told me her life story, and it was a hard one. Once her diabetes was under control, she prepared for her priest to come and stay at her house for a week.

Jesus loved the old Jewish man who had Parkinson's disease. He knew that he was getting progressively worse. Even with the help of his aide, it was getting harder and harder for him to use the new walk-in tub his son had built for him.

Jesus loved the man who loved another man but died of HIV/AIDS.

Jesus loved the woman who had her child taken away due to her addiction.

Jesus loved the woman who had every bone broken by her husband, a drug lord.

Jesus loved the biker woman who had breast cancer. She now attended every funeral for every biker killed in an accident.

I heard Father F. tell a story about when he was teaching at a college, which he has done for thirty years now. He goes on to say that the subject of being gay came up, and one student called it every disgusting, vulgar name under the sun. The whole class was up in arms, and that student had to apologize to the class. Afterward one student came up to Father and said, "I was very offended by what that student said, not because I am gay but because my older brother was and he wound up committing suicide." Judge not, lest you be judged (Matthew 7:2).

I came across something Billy Graham had said, "It is God's job to judge, The Holy Spirit's job to convict and our job to LOVE.

God's job ✝ to judge
Holy Spirit's ✝ job to
Convict ✝ and
Our ✝ job
To ✝ Love.

We are called to "Love One Another," not Judge One Another.

This is what Agape Love means. To love without judging, without contingencies, without expecting anything in return, to love just to love.

*I give you a new commandment: love one another. As I have loved you, so you also should love one another*
(John 13:34 NABRE)

We are all just children of God, and we need to start treating each other that way.

I love my children so very much. My prayer for them is that one day they will have a relationship with Jesus Christ as I do. I've told them that I love them so much that I cannot imagine going to heaven without knowing I will see them there. It may take some time. I wasn't into the Bible when I was young. It took years to come around. But I did, as I hope they will too one day. Just remember we all sinners, and my sin is no greater or lesser than yours. He loved and died for us when we were all still sinners, not saints! "We all fall short of the glory of God" (Romans 3:23 NABRE). That is why Jesus Christ died for us, to redeem us because our sin was great, but His love was greater. He made a way for us to be able to repent for our sins, be forgiven, and still go to heaven. I wrote in my journal:

> *Love comes in many forms:*
> *Love comes in the form of a kiss.*
> *Love comes in the form of giving of yourself.*
> *Love comes in the form of just being there for that person.*
> *Love comes in the form of helping one another physically, emotionally, or spiritually.*
> *Love comes in the form of expending your time, money, or energy, on someone else other than yourself.*
> *Love comes in the form of doing "the little things".*
> *Love comes in the form of saying, "I'm sorry" or "I love you".*
> *Love comes in the form of forgiving that person who has hurt you.*
> *Forgiveness comes out of love. You cannot forgive without love. You must love enough to forgive as Jesus did.*

I've heard it said, "Jesus forgives the one who loves the most." He came for the murderers, the liars, the pretenders, the cheats, the thieves, the adulterers, the abusers, the addicts, all the sinners—like you and me. He came to sacrifice His life for all sinners so that we may be forgiven and one day be in heaven with God the Father and Himself and the Holy Spirit.

You do not need to wait for the other person to say they are sorry. You must learn to forgive them, anyway. "...forgive us our trespasses as we forgive those who trespass against us" (Matthew 6:12 NABRE). Jesus didn't say, "Well, you can wait for an apology." Jesus said, "Forgive seventy times seven times."

Pope John Paul ll went to the prison to forgive Agca, the man who shot him in the Vatican Square in 1981.[128] The man didn't ask to be forgiven.

Immaculee' Ilibagdaza forgave the people who murdered her family in the Rwandan genocide.[129]

Louis Zamperini, after he was saved, forgave the Japanese guard who tortured him in the prison camp.[130]

---

128  "Pope John Paul II." 2020.
129  Immaculee Ilibagiza. 2006.
130  Louis Silvie Zamperini—American WW ll veteran, Christian evangelical, and Olympic distance runner in movie "Unbroken: Path to Redemption," 2018, Merritt Patterson Movie directed by Harold Cronk from a screenplay by Richard Friedberg and Ken Hixon, based on book by Laura Hillenbrand. ("Louis Zamperini." 2020. *Wikipedia, The Free Encyclopedia*. 2020. https://en.wikipedia.org/wiki/Louis_Zamperini.).

I've finally learned to forgive myself. It's a process. It's one of the hardest things to do. "Learning to love yourself is the greatest love of all," sang Whitney Houston.[131] It may as well be true. Without the love of God, oneself, and one another, how can we learn to forgive?

I think that learning to forgive yourself is harder than forgiving someone else. An example of this is when I couldn't afford to have my son Ronnie come home from college for Thanksgiving. It was $50 each way for the ferry, and I just didn't have it. I regret to this day that he had to spend Thanksgiving alone in his dorm when all the other kids went home. Or that one summer, I had left my son Jonathan at home because I was out with my boyfriend. It's times like these that forgiving yourself is the hardest thing to do. We all make mistakes, and to err is human, but to forgive oneself is really tough.

When you cannot forgive, you only hurt yourself. The other person doesn't even know you are upset usually. It's not bothering them one bit. They're not the ones who can't sleep at night thinking about it. They're not the ones who are angry about it. They're not the ones taking it out on something or someone else. They're not the ones getting sick over it. I've heard Pastor Joseph

131 "The Greatest Love of All." 2020. *Wikipedia, The Free Encyclopedia.* 2020. https://en.wikipedia.org/wiki/The_Greatest_Love_of_All.

Prince say, "Let Go and Let GOD."[132] Easier said than done sometimes. But the release of all the hurt and all the emotions that go with it when you do, is so freeing! When you forgive someone else, you feel as if a heavy burden has been taken off of your shoulders. It is such a good feeling that once you've done it, you will be able to do it again more readily.

In the same way, we should ask God to forgive us of our sins. If we are truly sorry and try to do better, we will be forgiven. Our sins have been paid for in full by Jesus Christ. He loved us enough to die for us. The St. Francis of Assisi Prayer is one that I've hung onto since a teenager. I say it often:

*Lord, make me an instrument of your peace;*
*Where there is hatred let me sow Love;*
*Where there is injury, pardon;*
*Where there is Doubt, faith;*
*Where there is despair, hope ;*
*Where there is darkness, light; and*
*Where there is sadness, joy.*
*O Divine Master,*
*Grant that I may not so much seek*
*To be consoled as to console;*
*To be understood as to understand;*

---

132 "Joseph Prince." 2020. *Wikipedia, The Free Encyclopedia.* 2020. https://en.wikipedia.org/wiki/Joseph_Prince.

*To be loved as to love;*
*For it is in giving that we receive;*
*It is in pardoning that we are pardoned;*
*And it is in dying that we are to born to eternal life.*[133]

---

133  St. Francis of Assisi Prayer—although commonly attributed to St. Francis of Assisi (1181–1226) the prayer can be traced back later than 1912 when it appeared in a French spiritual magazine called La Clochette. It was published by a Catholic association called La Ligue de la Sainte-Messe, "The Holy Mass League" founded in 1901 by a French priest, Father Esther Bouquerel (1855–1923). It bore the title of Belle priere a faire pendant la messe. A Beautiful Prayer to say During the Mass' and was published anonymously. St. Francis may not have written the words of the prayer attributed to him but he certainly lived them ("A Closer Look at the Peace Prayer of Saint Francis." n.d. Franciscan Media. 2020. https://www.franciscanmedia.org/a-closer-look-at-the-peace-prayer-of-saint-francis/.).

# CHAPTER 10

# The End?

The End?

Or is it just the beginning?

Jesus taught us that life is everlasting, not this one but the one to come (John 11:25–26). Because He gave His life for us and shed His blood for our salvation (Revelation 1:5). If you only believe, you too can live (John 11:25). He rose from the dead after three days as he promised (John 20:17). He also promises us a place up in heaven with Him and the Father when we die (John 14:2).

This is the hope for you, me, and all mankind. But this isn't "all there is". This imperfect world, with all its evil, all its brokenness, unfairness, pain, and sorrow... There's got to be more! We deserve more! We've been on the devil's playing field for far too long (1 Peter 5:8). Jesus is coming again to make things right to make a heaven on earth, and the devil and his armies are all going straight to hell (Revelation 21:1–2, 20:10). And you can take that to the bank!

That reminds me of a joke the priest told one Sunday. It was about a woman who thought she was a very devout Catholic, she gave to the poor, went to mass every week, and she thought surely she was going straight to heaven when she died. Well, when she died, she did go to heaven. She greets St. Peter at the gate, and he allows her entry into heaven. But to her surprise, she sees her mother-in-law, her ex-husband, her neighbor down the block whom she didn't get along with, but not one of them said a word. She thought, *Is heaven silent?* So, she goes back over to see St. Peter and asks, "St. Peter, why are all the people silent here?" St. Peter looks at her and finally replies, "They're not silent; they're just in shock to see you here."

The moral of the story is

1) Don't judge others.

2) Don't think of yourself as holier than art thou.

And...

3) You will be surprised who you meet in heaven.

When Jesus comes again, all knees shall bow to Him and know that He is Lord (Romans 14:11). He has made saints out of sinners and sinners into saints. He dined with Zacchaeus (Luke 19:5). He cast out seven demons from Mary Magdalene and still felt she was worthy of his teachings (Luke 8:2). He drank water from the cup of a Samaritan woman (John 4:7). He planted His church on the rock, Peter, the same person who denied him publicly, not once, but three times (Matthew 16:18, 27:75). He appeared to the man, Saul, who was killing all Christians, and He died for sinners like you and me (Acts 9:5). On April 23, 2018, I wrote:

> *Lord, you make*
> *The weak—strong,*
> *The blind—see*
> *The deaf—hear*
> *The prideful—humble*
> *The unqualified—qualified*
> *The scarred—beautiful*
> *The lonely—wanted*
> *The unlovable—loved*
> *The sad—happy*
> *The forgotten—remembered*
> *The sinner—forgiven.*

Do we grieve when a loved one dies? Yes. But we grieve with hope. Hope that we will see them again and that they are in a better place, namely heaven. It doesn't make death any easier for the family and loved ones left on this side of heaven, though. We miss them terribly because we loved them. We miss their laugh, their smile, their hugs, their love, their humanness, what made them, them. Most of us have lost someone we've loved to death, and it's not a good feeling for us. But it may be for them! That's the ironic part of it all. There's the old saying, "They are in a better place now." Are they? If they had a relationship with the Lord this side of heaven, we can almost be certain they will have a relationship with the lord on the other side as well. I wrote:

> *When someone we love dies:*
> *It's always the hardest to say "goodbye"...*
> *But that loved one lives on*
> *In spirit through love*
> *That stays deep within our hearts.*
> *Love knows no space,*
> *No time,*
> *No distance,*
> *Love lives ON...*
> *You cannot kill love,*
> *Because love never dies,*
> *Even if the earth and stars pass away,*
> *One thing will always remain...*
> *Love.*

One of the hardest things I've had to do was watch one of my best friends, Tee, fight colon cancer, which had spread to her lungs and bones in the two years she fought to live. I miss her. We used to go to the movies, street fairs, bars, road trips to Greenport, the wineries, dancing, the beach, music festivals, parties, work, and weddings together. We went to chemotherapy together and then lunch if she felt well enough.

On January 11, 2019, I saw my friend dying in hospice. She was heavily medicated for pain. I had just been released from the hospital the day before after my hip replacement and asked my youngest sister, Marlene, to drive me. She was awake, and she spoke to me. I told her that I wanted to see her before God forbid anything happened, and I wouldn't be able to forgive myself.

I said, "Tee, we at my Bible group have been praying for you to find peace. Have you found it yet?"

She hesitated a minute (for she knew I didn't mean the peace as the world knows it but His peace that surpasses all understanding, John 14:27) and then said, "Yes."

I said, "Tee, you look so tired."

She said, "I am."

I replied, "Tee, you've fought the good fight for a long time now, and you've suffered enough, and Jesus knows your pain, and enough is enough. He hung on that cross for us," and as I was telling her, tears are just rolling down my face.

I said, "Tee, the Lord has many rooms prepared for us, and I think that you will be re-decorating a new room for yourself in His house." (She had just decorated a room to stay in her daughter's house).

She said, "I just want to go in my sleep."

I said, "We've discussed this already."

And she said, "Yes, we have."

I then said, "When the time comes, the Lord will send His legion of angels with Our Lady to take you to heaven."[134]

She said, "I hope so."

I said, "I know so."

The aide who came in said, "And I have Jesus Christ on speed dial," and we laughed.

She told me, "I love you so very, very, very, very much."

Now, I'm not even trying to keep it together anymore, I said, "I do too, but (pointing to heaven) He Loves you more."

She then told me that the bed next to her was for family members to sleep over on. I told her if I wasn't just operated on that I would have stayed with her in that other bed. I told her that I would be praying for her and that I would try to come back tomorrow. I told her I loved her. That was the last time I saw her. I could

---

134 Our Lady- often refers to Mary, mother of Jesus, in the Veneration of Mary in the Catholic Church.

not return the next day because I was in too much pain with my hip. I called her daughter and asked her to please tell her that I couldn't come and the reason why.

On January 12, 2016, another one of my friends, Judy, went to see her, and she said that she looked like her mom did before she died. She said that Tee did not speak a word to her. January 13, 2019, I found out through another friend that her daughter and son were with her today, and she did not open her eyes but knew they were there. Her daughter texted me and said her breathing is labored, and she has a fever. I asked her daughter, "Will someone be with her tonight?" I did not want her to die alone. Her daughter assured me that her brother would stay the night.

The next day another friend of mine went to see her. She said, "She did not speak to us, but she was aware that we were there." I've been praying for her to pass in her sleep like she wants to. I prayed in the Spirit to give her the courage and strength to die. She can rest now. She sold her condominium, made all her own funeral arrangements, and bought her space in the mausoleum at St. Charles' cemetery. She went to confession, and was anointed with Last Rites; not too many of us get to do all that![135]

I went humbly but boldly to the throne of God to ask for a miracle for Tee. And I was always expecting one. But... it was not God's plan for a miracle nor His will. She has a relationship with the Lord, and I think she now prays just to go home. I pray He will show her mercy and not let her suffer much longer.

On January 18, 2019, it was morning, and I heard the song come on the radio, *I Can Only Imagine* by Mercy Me.[136] As I sang this song, sobbing between versus, I said, "Tee, this one's for you." Unbeknownst to me, she had passed during the night. I had played that song for her when we were driving to chemotherapy.

On January 19, 2019, I mourn the death of my dear friend, Tee. To some, she was a mom, a sister, a nurse, a supervisor, a neighbor, a coworker, but to me, she was just my friend. My "Hey, Girlfriend." We'd laugh, cry, dance, talk, listen, give advice, and just be there for each other. She was my confidante, my fun-loving,

---

135 Last Rites— "in Catholicism, are the last prayers and ministrations given to an individual of the faith, when possible, shortly before death. Anointing of the sick is generally accompanied with the celebration of the sacraments of Penance and Viaticum(Holy Communion)" ("Last Rites." 2020. *Wikipedia, The Free Encyclopedia*. 2020. https://en.wikipedia.org/wiki/Last_rites.).
136 "I can only Imagine" song by Christian rock band Mercy Me on the "The Almost There" album, released October 12, 2001 written by Bart Millard, produced by Pete Kipley.

hanging out with buddy, my tell-all to with no secrets barred friend, my make plans with and dream dreams with friend.

We were able to have those uncomfortable talks about God and our relationship with Him and the afterlife. I am sure that God has welcomed home his daughter into heaven into His loving arms.

I am but a selfish person, as I miss my "girlfriend" already. But I am entitled to my tears... Didn't Jesus weep for his friend Lazarus when he died (John 11:35)? My rational mind tells me she's in a better place with no more suffering. I imagine the Lord saying, "Welcome home, my dear daughter, you've run the course, you've finished the race." She fought the good fight for as long as she could. She knows how much I loved her. She will remain in my heart forever. So, I'm here to say goodbye, until we meet again, to one of my best friends, Tee, whom I loved.

So, I know death is not the end. I think of it as a new beginning, a new chapter to a new life. One without any pain, sorrow, guilt, or sin. One of complete joy—So complete that we humans cannot even fathom it.

Do I still miss her? You bet I do. Do I think I will see her again? You bet I do. Do I still pray for her?

Yes, I do, although I think she's in a better position to pray for me.

Jesus Christ will come again at the end of time. End of this world, not His. He will come again to bring a new heaven onto a new earth, as Revelation says (21:10).

So, Tee, as I sit here on your bench and remember you, and pray for you, you'll be happy to know that I'm almost done with writing His book that I told you about. You'll also be surprised that you are in it!

The End?

No. For you see, love never ends. Love never dies. For God is love. I think it's only just the beginning, my friends.

So, in conclusion:

You see that you can live outside the box, outside the world's norm, out of the darkness into the light, expecting miracles in everyday life, dreaming big dreams, knowing that with God all things are possible. You can live your life, with love, in Christ Jesus, knowing there is no end if only you just... Believe.

# Epilogue

As I am proofreading this book, the COVID-19 virus outbreak is happening. This may be your desert storm. You may be quarantined at home; you may be working from home, some have your children at home with you. You may be afraid that you've come in contact with someone who has the virus; maybe you're afraid your parents or your children will get the disease. Maybe you're afraid you may even get the disease and possibly die or see one of your loved ones die. Maybe you're afraid you won't have enough money to feed your family or pay the rent. I know these are real fears, and frankly, it's scary as hell. I'd be lying if I didn't admit to sharing some of these same fears. Whatever is going on in your storm walk right now, know that prayer and realizing that "God is still on the throne," as Max Lucado said. He may well be our only hope as well as our only answer to this "unprecedented event".

I hope you, like myself, are praying more and realizing that just because "churches" are closed, God still hears the prayers of the many. Wherever or whoever you are, no matter which congregation you may belong to, pray. We need to change our ways and ask for forgiveness.

This world needed a "time-out" to get off that "merry-go-round" of life, as we once knew. The whirlwind of running to get to work on time, go food shopping, taking the kids to extra curriculum activities, making dinner, doing homework, cleaning up, and finally trying to get some sleep. We needed to STOP and look around at what we're doing, what we have done, not only to mother earth, nature but to ourselves and our children. The "rat race" has gotten too many anxious, depressed, stressed out, sleep-deprived people. The slave trafficking, abortion, pornography, addictions, road rages, murders, rapes, shootings, punching out of the elderly on streets and robbing them, gangs, and the list goes on and on.

We are now forced to stay at home with our families, with all the comforts of home, and somehow we don't think we will be able to do just that! We are not being sent off to concentration camps; we're not being asked to go to war. We are being asked to sit home on our couches with all the modern commodities at our disposal. We're being asked to talk to one another again, to pray together, share meals together, like in the "old days," to be there for one another face to face. Thank

God we live in an era that has internet and Zoom and Skype and face time. I don't know about you, but it's too early to know how many of us may die from this, but I am sure that I'd want to spend every moment I have left with the ones I love the most. I realize that it is not possible for some of us because our adult children and loved ones live in other states.

I'm not saying that these times are easy by any means. The wearing of a mask, the social distancing, the loneliness, especially for those with mental illness and those living alone. It is a trying time, not doing what we call "routine" or "normal" anymore. There's a general anxiety in the air; I'm sure everyone feels it to some degree. It's the not knowing the "when's" or the "what if's" or the "how long's". It's all the uncertainties of who, where, when, and why that cannot be answered. Believe me, I get it. My mother is in a nursing home, and they have twenty-five patients that have COVID-19; seven employees, and one death thus far. It's sad because we cannot visit her and she has some dementia, and she doesn't remember why we are not coming to see her. What the worst thing is... I cannot get in to see her or to help her. I don't think anyone deserves to die alone. People in nursing homes, group homes, adult homes are really at the mercy of their caregivers and God. I pray that He watches over those unable to watch out for themselves and for the ones who are dying and for those who have died and their families. May God be with them and have mercy on them.

There is a lot of good coming from this as well. When September 11th happened here in N.Y., people came from all over the nation to help. People went back to church. People called on and relied on God again. People are once more stepping up to the plate to help. People are giving to the food pantries, the restaurant owners making hot food for the poor, fast food places giving free food to the "essential workers," individuals donating what masks and gloves they have to the hospitals when they were so very short on PPE supplies. Individuals were sewing masks at home; one person donated the 2,000 masks she made on her sewing machine. Others have devised masks from 3-D printers. Factory workers from automobiles companies have been making respirators instead of cars. One doctor figured out a way to make a Bi-pap machines into ventilators; others have been finding ways to use one ventilator for two people. Retired nurses and doctors were asked to come out of retirement, and 30,000 of them have answered Gov. Cuomo's call. Samaritan's purse, a nonprofit evangelistic organization, came and set up tents in Central Park equipped with doctors and nurses and supplies. The Navy ship USS Comfort was sent by President Trump to aid with the overflow of city hospitals until the peak of the pandemic was over. It is a beautiful thing to see people banding together for the good of all. I hope this is the start of a Christian revival. And the earth is healing. The hole in the ozone layer has closed. The skies are blue again, the air is smog-free, the waters are cleaner. I think God makes a way when we don't see a way.

The front-line workers, the nurses, the aides, the EMT's, the doctors, the ambulance drivers, all essential workers that are all sacrificing their lives on a daily basis, God bless them. But, as I've been seeing and hearing, this is leaving an indelible scar on these health care workers. I can only hope and pray that some with PTSD are experiencing because of the many deaths here in N.Y. can be relieved in some way and that they will be able to get the resources they need. I pray for these people that God continues to give them the strength and courage they require for such a time as this.

As a Christian, I know there is a place reserved for me in heaven. I just worry about my loved ones I will leave behind. I have to trust in God and His will, because His will, will be done. I pray that I will not have to bury any of my family or friends. Just remember friends, that God is in control. My prayer for you is that you find God and surrender your hearts to Him. Find peace. Love one another. *Live Outside The Box.* Trust and, most of all... Believe.

Live
Faith over Fear,
Peace over Pandemonium,
Prayer over Pandemics,
Live
Worship over worry,
Love over Loneliness,
Joy over Judgement,
Hope over hopelessness,
Live
as Christ did for He has
already
Won the War.

# References

"A Closer Look at the Peace Prayer of Saint Francis."
2020. Franciscan Media. 2020. https://www.franciscanmedia.org/a-closer-look-at-the-peace-prayer-of-saint-francis/.

"Afters - I Will Fear No More Lyrics by Joshua Havens,
Jason Ingram, Jordan Mohilowski, Matt Fuqua, and
Dan Ostebo -2018." n.d. Metrolyrics. 2020. https://
www.metrolyrics.com/i-will-fear-no-more-lyrics-afters.html.

"Amazing Grace." 2020. *Wikipedia, The Free Encyclopedia*. 2020. https://en.wikipedia.org/wiki/
Amazing_Grace.

"Augustine Quote." 2019. Fauxtations Wordpress. 2019.
https://fauxtations.wordpress.com/2019/08/29/
augustine-god-loves-each-of-us/.

"Beautifully Broken by Tiffany Arbuckle Lee, and Jenny
Slate Lee, 2018." n.d. *Wikipedia, The Free Encyclopedia*. https://en.wikipedia.org/wiki/Plumb_(singer).

"Behind The Song: Matthew West Shares The Story Behind The Song 'The God Who Stays.'" 2019. Freeccm.Com. 2019. https://freeccm.com/2019/10/29/behind-the-song-matthew-west-shares-the-story-behind-the-song-the-god-who-stays/.

"Billy Graham." 2020. *Wikipedia, The Free Encyclopedia.* 2020. https://en.wikipedia.org/wiki/Billy_Graham.

"Billy Graham." 2020. *Wikipedia, The Free Encyclopedia.* 2020. https://en.wikipedia.org/wiki/Billy_Graham.

"Bishop Robert Barron - Word on Fire." n.d. YouTube. 2020. https://www.youtube.com/channel/UCcMjLgeWNwqL2LBGS-iPb1A.

"Carl Sagan." 2020. *Wikipedia, The Free Encyclopedia.* 2020. https://en.wikipedia.org/wiki/Carl_Sagan.

"Carrie Underwood 'Jesus Take the Wheel,' 2005." 2020. *Wikipedia, The Free Encyclopedia.* 2020. https://www.musicnotes.com/sheetmusic/mtd.asp?ppn=MN0053248.

"Christine Caine." 2020. *Wikipedia, The Free Encyclopedia.* 2020. https://en.wikipedia.org/wiki/Christine_Caine.

"Citizen Way - I Will Lyrics, Written by Ben Calhoun and Jeff Pardo, Released 2016." n.d. Azlyrics.Com. 2020. https://www.azlyrics.com/lyrics/citizenway/iwill.html.

"Definition of Blessing." 2020. Dictionary.Com. 2020. https://www.dictionary.com/browse/blessing?s=t.

"Desert." 2020. Merriam-Webster Online Dictionary. Merriam-Webster, Incorporated. 2020. https://www.merriam-webster.com/dictionary/desert.

"Drawn To You by Audrey Assad, 2018." n.d. AZLyrics. Com. 2020. https://www.azlyrics.com/lyrics/audreyassad/drawntoyou.html.

"Dymphna." 2020. *Wikipedia, The Free Encyclopedia.* 2020. https://en.wikipedia.org/wiki/Dymphna.

"Father Cedric Pisegna Ministries- Houston Texas." 2006. Www.Frcedric.Org. 2006. https://frcedric.org/default.aspx?MenuItemID=174&MenuGroup=Public+Home.

"Footprints in the Sand (Poem)." 2020. *Wikipedia, The Free Encyclopedia.* 2020. https://en.wikipedia.org/wiki/Talk%3AFootprints_(poem).

"Franklin D. Roosevelt." 2020. *Wikipedia, The Free Encyclopedia.* 2020. https://en.wikipedia.org/wiki/Franklin_D._Roosevelt.

"God Friended Me." 2020. *Wikipedia, The Free Encyclopedia.* 2020. https://en.wikipedia.org/wiki/God_Friended_Me.

"Grace in Christianity." 2020. *Wikipedia, The Free Encyclopedia.* 2020. https://en.wikipedia.org/wiki/Grace_in_Christianity.

"Hacksaw Ridge." 2020. *Wikipedia, The Free Encyclopedia.* https://en.wikipedia.org/wiki/Hacksaw_Ridge.

"Henri Nouwen." 2020. *Wikipedia, The Free Encyclopedia*. 2020. https://en.wikipedia.org/wiki/Henri_Nouwen.

"Henry Ford." 2020. *Wikipedia, The Free Encyclopedia*. 2020. https://en.wikipedia.org/wiki/Henry_Ford.

"If the Magi Were Women..." 2020. Beliefnet. 2020. https://www.beliefnet.com/entertainment/video-jokes/jokes/christian/i/if-the-magi-were-women.aspx.

"Jesus Loves Me, This I Know by Anna Bartlett Warner." 2020. Hymnary.Org. 2020. https://hymnary.org/text/jesus_loves_me_this_i_know_for_the_bible.

"Joan of Arc." 2020. *Wikipedia, The Free Encyclopedia*. 2020. https://en.wikipedia.org/wiki/Joan_of_Arc.

"Joel Osteen – Become a Miracle." 2014. Sermonly. 2014. http://www.sermonly.com/14/joel-osteen-become-a-miracle/7014/.

"Joseph F. Girzone." 2020. *Wikipedia, The Free Encyclopedia*. 2020. https://en.wikipedia.org/wiki/Joseph_F._Girzone.

"Joseph Prince." 2020. *Wikipedia, The Free Encyclopedia*. 2020. https://en.wikipedia.org/wiki/Joseph_Prince.

"Josephine Bakhita." 2020. *Wikipedia, The Free Encyclopedia*. 2020. https://en.wikipedia.org/wiki/Josephine_Bakhita.

"Kanye West." 2020. *Wikipedia, The Free Encyclopedia.* 2020. https://en.wikipedia.org/wiki/Kanye_West.

"Last Rites." 2020. *Wikipedia, The Free Encyclopedia.* 2020. https://en.wikipedia.org/wiki/Last_rites.

"Living Beyond Blessed by Pastor Robert Morris: Gateway Church." 2019. Gateway Church. 2019. https://gatewaypeople.com/series/beyond-blessed.

"Louis Zamperini." 2020. *Wikipedia, The Free Encyclopedia.* 2020. https://en.wikipedia.org/wiki/Louis_Zamperini.

"Lyrics for Joy by For King & Country, 2018." 2020. Song Facts. 2020. https://www.songfacts.com/lyrics/for-king-country/joy.

"Martin Luther King Jr." 2020. *Wikipedia, The Free Encyclopedia.* 2020. https://en.wikipedia.org/wiki/Martin_Luther_King_Jr.

"Matt Hammitt - Tears Lyrics, 2017." n.d. Azlyrics.Com. 2020. https://www.azlyrics.com/lyrics/matthammitt/tears.html.

"Matthew and Laurie Crouch." 2020. *Wikipedia, The Free Encyclopedia.* 2020. https://en.wikipedia.org/wiki/Special:Search?search=%09Matthew+and+Laurie+Crouch&go=Go&nso=1.

"Matthew West - Do Something Lyrics, 2012." n.d. Azlyrics.Com. 2020. https://www.azlyrics.com/lyrics/matthewwest/dosomething.html.

"Maximilian Kolbe." 2020. *Wikipedia, The Free Encyclopedia.* 2020. https://en.wikipedia.org/wiki/ Maximilian_Kolbe.

"Miracle of the Sun, Fatima, Portugal, October 13, 1917." 2020. *Wikipedia, The Free Encyclopedia.* 2020. https://en.wikipedia.org/wiki/Miracle_of_the_Sun.

"Miracle." n.d. Oxford Reference. 2020. https:// www.oxfordreference.com/view/10.1093/oi/ authority.20110803100200612.

"Mother Teresa Quote." n.d. Quotefancy. 2020. https:// quotefancy.com/quote/868994/Mother-Teresa-I-am-nothing-I-am-but-an-instrument-a-tiny-pencil-in-the-hands-of-the-Lord.

"Mother Teresa." 2020. *Wikipedia, The Free Encyclopedia.* 2020. https://en.wikipedia.org/wiki/ Mother_Teresa.

"Nick Vujicic." 2020. *Wikipedia, The Free Encyclopedia.* 2020. https://en.wikipedia.org/wiki/Nick_Vujicic.

"Our Lady of Guadalupe." 2020. *Wikipedia, The Free Encyclopedia.* 2020. https://en.wikipedia.org/wiki/ Our_Lady_of_Guadalupe.

"Our Lady of Lourdes." 2020. *Wikipedia, The Free Encyclopedia.* 2020. https://en.wikipedia.org/wiki/ Our_Lady_of_Lourdes.

"Paul Harvey and 'The Man and the Birds.' Posted 2019." 2020. Christian Heritage Fellowship, Inc.

2020. https://christianheritagefellowship.com/paul-harvey-and-the-man-and-the-birds/.

"Pope Francis." 2020. *Wikipedia, The Free Encyclopedia.* 2020. https://en.wikipedia.org/wiki/Pope_Francis.

"Pope Francis." 2020. *Wikipedia, The Free Encyclopedia.* 2020. https://en.wikipedia.org/wiki/Pope_Francis.

"Pope John Paul II." 2020. *Wikipedia, The Free Encyclopedia.* 2020. https://en.wikipedia.org/wiki/Pope_John_Paul_II.

"Priscilla Shirer." 2020. *Wikipedia, The Free Encyclopedia.* 2020. https://en.wikipedia.org/wiki/Priscilla_Shirer.

"Quote by Albert Einstein." n.d. Goodreads, Inc. 2020. https://www.goodreads.com/quotes/987-there-are-only-two-ways-to-live-your-life-one.

"Quote by Anonymous: 'You Can Never out-Give God.'" n.d. Goodreads.Com. 2020. https://www.goodreads.com/quotes/7389609-you-can-never-out-give-god.

"Quote by C.S. Lewis." n.d. Goodreads, Inc. 2020. https://www.goodreads.com/quotes/623193-we-can-ignore-even-pleasure-but-pain-insists-upon-being.

"Quote by Francis de Sales." 2020. Goodreads, Inc. 2020. https://www.goodreads.com/quotes/32909-the-measure-of-love-is-to-love-without-measure.

"Quote by Franklin Delano Roosevelt." 2020. Goodreads, Inc. 2020. https://www.goodreads.com/

quotes/1017824-we-have-always-held-to-the-hope-the-belief-the.

"Quote by Joe Stowell, ODB: The Great Creator-Healer." 2014. Why Am I [YMI]: Our Daily Bread Ministries. 2014. https://ymi.today/2014/02/odb-the-great-creator-healer/.

"Quote by Martin Luther King Jr." 2020. Goodreads, Inc. 2020. https://www.goodreads.com/quotes/37292-we-must-accept-finite-disappoint-ment-but-never-lose-infinite-hope.

"Quote by Mother Teresa." 2016. Catholic News Service. 2016. https://www.catholicnews.com/services/englishnews/2016/mother-teresa-do-small-things-with-great-love.cfm.

"Quote by Mother Teresa." 2020. Goodreads, Inc. 2020. https://www.goodreads.com/quotes/153541-intense-love-does-not-measure-it-just-gives.

"Quote by Saint Augustine of Hippo." 2020. Goodreads, Inc. 2020. https://www.goodreads.com/quotes/24726-love-is-the-beauty-of-the-soul.

"Quote by Saint Augustine." 2020. Goodreads, Inc. 2020. https://www.goodreads.com/quotes/32262-faith-is-to-believe-what-you-do-not-yet-see.

"Rabbi Schneider, Shaliach – A Jewish Messenger Of Jesus." 2020. Discovering the Jewish Jesus. 2020. https://discoveringthejewishjesus.com/about-2/rabbi-schneider/.

"Robert Morris, Gateway Church (Texas)." 2020. *Wikipedia, The Free Encyclopedia.* March 9, 2020. http://gatewaypeople.com/profiles/robert-morris.

"Saint Patrick." 2020. *Wikipedia, The Free Encyclopedia.* 2020. https://en.wikipedia.org/wiki/Saint_Patrick.

"Serenity Prayer by Reinhold Niebuhr, 1951." 2020. *Wikipedia, The Free Encyclopedia.* 2020. https://en.wikipedia.org/wiki/Serenity_Prayer.

"Sidewalk Prophets - Smile Lyrics, 2019." 2020. Azlyrics.Com. 2020. https://www.azlyrics.com/lyrics/sidewalkprophets/smile.html.

"Steven Furtick." 2020. *Wikipedia, The Free Encyclopedia.* 2020. https://en.wikipedia.org/wiki/Steven_Furtick.

"Storm." 2020. Merriam-Webster Online Dictionary. Merriam-Webster, Incorporated. 2020. https://www.merriam-webster.com/dictionary/storm.

"Surrounded (Fight My Battles) Lyrics by Michael W. Smith, Released 2018." n.d. AZLyrics.Com. 2020. https://www.azlyrics.com/lyrics/upperroom/surroundedfightmybattles757618.html.

"Synesthesia." 2020. Psychology Today. 2020. https://www.psychologytoday.com/us/basics/synesthesia.

"The Greatest Love of All." 2020. *Wikipedia, The Free Encyclopedia.* 2020. https://en.wikipedia.org/wiki/The_Greatest_Love_of_All.

"The Greatest Man in History - A Poem by Lyle C. Rollings III, 2007." 2017. All Poetry. 2017. https://allpoetry.com/poem/13046422-The-Greatest-Man-In-History--by-Warofli.

"The Passion of The Christ - Jim Caviezel (Complete Interview)." 2013. Catholic Inside USA YouTube. 2013. https://www.youtube.com/channel/UCE1gMy-ucEoA7C5TtBN0PPg.

"The Passion of the Christ, Co-Written and Directed by Mel Gibson, Released February 25, 2004." 2020. *Wikipedia, The Free Encyclopedia.* 2020. https://en.wikipedia.org/wiki/The_Passion_of_the_Christ.

"The Shack Movie, Based on the Novel by William Paul Young." n.d. Lionsgate.Com. 2020. https://www.lionsgate.com/movies/the-shack.

"The Star Thrower by Loren Eisely, 1969." 2019. *Wikipedia, The Free Encyclopedia.* 2019. https://en.wikipedia.org/wiki/The_Star_Thrower.

"Thomas Edison." 2020. *Wikipedia, The Free Encyclopedia.* 2020. https://en.wikipedia.org/wiki/Thomas_Edison.

"Unbroken (Film) - Wikipedia." 2020. *Wikipedia, The Free Encyclopedia.* 2020. https://en.wikipedia.org/wiki/Unbroken_(film).

"World Population Clock: 7.8 Billion People (2020)." 2020. Worldometers.Info. 2020. https://www.worldometers.info/world-population/.

"Wright Brothers." 2020. *Wikipedia, The Free Encyclopedia*. 2020. https://en.wikipedia.org/wiki/Wright_brothers.

*21st Century King James Version [KJ21]*. 1994. Gary, SD: Deuel Enterprises, Inc. https://www.biblegateway.com/versions/21st-Century-King-James-Version-KJ21-Bible/.

Alexandra, Tanner. 2018. "The Lion, the Witch and the Wardrobe Study Guide, Literature Guide." LitCharts LLC. 2018. https://www.litcharts.com/lit/the-lion-the-witch-and-the-wardrobe.

Batterson, Mark. 2016. *The Circle Maker*. Zondervan. https://www.christianbook.com/the-circle-maker-mark-batterson/9780310346913/pd/346913.

Cahn, Jonathan. 2012. *The Harbinger: The Ancient Mystery That Holds the Secret of America's Future*. Frontline.

Chapman, Marina. 2013. *The Girl With No Name: The Incredible True Story of a Child Raised by Monkeys*. Pegasus. https://www.goodreads.com/book/show/16102341-the-girl-with-no-name.

*Evangelical Heritage Version [EHV]*. 2019. Wartburg Project. https://www.biblegateway.com/versions/Evangelical-Heritage-Version-EHV-Bible/.

Franklin, Jentezen. 2018. *Love Like You've Never Been Hurt: Hope, Healing and the Power of an Open Heart*.

Bloomington, Minnesota: Chosen Books, a Division of Baker Publishing Group.

Immaculee Ilibagiza. 2006. *Left to Tell: Discovering God Amidst the Rwandan Holocaust.* Hay House.

Kelly, Matthew. 2015. *Rediscover Jesus: An Invitation.* Beacon Publishing. https://www.goodreads.com/book/show/27968974-rediscover-jesus.

Kelly, Matthew. 2015. *Rediscover Jesus: An Invitation.* Blue Sparrow, Beacon Publishing.

Kosicki, Rev. George W. 2003. *Divine Mercy Answers Life's Crises and Problem.* C.S.B. quotes from the Diary of St. Faustina used with permission of the Marians of the Immaculate Conception, Eden Hill, Stockbridge, MA. https://www.renewalministries.net/files/freeliterature/DM%20Answers%20life%20crises%20and%20problems.pdf

Lewis, C. S. 2001. *Mere Christianity.* New York, NY: Harper Collins.

Morris, Robert. 2016. *Frequency.* Thomas Nelson; First Edition first Printing (April 26, 2016). https://gatewaypeople.com/series/frequency-2016.

Stanley, Charles Frazier. Pastor emeritus of the First Baptist Church in Atlanta, Georgia, having been senior pastor for fifty-one years.

Tan, Rebecca, and Tania Dutta. 2019. "74-Year-Old Mangayamma Yaramati Gives Birth to Twins in India." The Washington Post. 2019. https://

www.washingtonpost.com/world/2019/09/06/
this-year-old-woman-just-gave-birth-twins/.

*The Good News Bible [GNT]*. n.d. New York:
American Bible Society. Public Domain.
https://www.biblegateway.com/versions/
Good-News-Translation-GNT-Bible/#booklist.

*The Holy Bible: English Standard Version [ESV]*.
2007. Wheaton, Ill: Crossway Bibles. Public domain. https://www.biblegateway.com/versions/
English-Standard-Version-ESV-Bible/#booklist.

*The Holy Bible: International Standard Ver-
sion [ISV]*. 2014. Davidson Press LLC.
https://www.biblegateway.com/versions/
International-Standard-Version-ISV-Bible/.

*The Holy Bible: King James Version [KJV]*. 1999. New York,
NY: American Bible Society. Public Domain.

*The Holy Bible: New American Bible (Revised Edition) Ver-
sion [NABRE]*. 2010. Bible Gateway. Washington:
Confraternity of Christian Doctrine, Inc. https://
www.biblegateway.com/versions/New-American-
Bible-Revised-Edition-NABRE-Bible/.

*The Holy Bible: New American Standard Bible [NASB]*.
1995. The Lockman Foundation. http://www.lock-
man.org/nasb/index.php.

*The Holy Bible: New International Version [NIV]*. 1984.
Grand Rapids: Zonderman Publishing House.

https://www.biblegateway.com/versions/ New-International-Version-NIV-Bible/#booklist.

*The Holy Bible: New Living Translation [NLT].* 2013. Carol Stream: Tyndale House Foundation. Tyndale House Publishers, Inc. https://www.biblegateway.com/versions/ New-Living-Translation-NLT-Bible/#booklist.

*The Holy Bible: The New King James Version [NKJV].* 1999. Nashville, TN: Thomas Nelson, Inc. https://www.biblegateway.com/versions/ New-King-James-Version-NKJV-Bible/#booklist.

# About the Author

I, Laura Riviezzo-Taggart, live on the eastern end of Long Island, New York, for the past thirty something years. Not the Hamptons, but just a modest home in a small town. I married in the 1980s and divorced in the 2000s. I have two adult sons, whom I love so much. I've worked as a psychiatric nurse on Long Island N.Y. for over forty years. I've worked in a state mental institution as well as a modern psychiatric emergency room in a big hospital. I've also worked in the community going into peoples' homes.

I've encountered the mentally ill, the depressed, the suicidal, victims of violence, the alcoholic, and the drug-addicted; the Aspergers, Autistic, and ADHD children, the mentally and physically handicapped, the Vietnam and Afghanistan veteran's PTSD and the 9/11 first responder's PTSD, and with death and dying... I've encountered the rich, the poor, the atheist, the agnostic, the believer. Mental challenges affect everyone; it knows no boundaries, no borders, no nationality, no race, nor creed. Sadly, all walks of life are included without any partiality.

God has given me a gift, not just to become a nurse. But to be a nurse who can reach into people's hearts and souls with compassion and empathy, lovingly listening to them, having them open up their hearts to me, sharing their deepest fears, and trusting me with their story. Together we try to find meaning, and if we're lucky, a solution. This has motivated me to help people, not just physically but emotionally and spiritually.

To have come this far in my own spiritual journey, I cannot remember a day I haven't asked or thanked God for His help. The people I've met, the friendships we have made, the experiences I've encountered, and the lessons I've learned about life, love, faith, hope, and death, have all prepared me to share this story as a testimony to the Glory of God.

I was brought up a Roman Catholic and remain one. I've been called a "Born-Again" Catholic. I pray, I read my Bible, I attend a nondenominational Bible group, attend mass weekly, go to confession, go on mission trips and retreats, give to the needy and to other worthwhile causes. I have an interpersonal relationship with my Lord, and I hear the Holy Spirit when He speaks to me. I believe in today's Christian artists. They are gifted, awe-inspiring musicians, Holy Spirit driven, and gospel influenced songwriters.

Many of TBN's Protestant/Evangelical pastors, like Robert Morris and Charles Stanley, David Jeremiah and Billy Graham, all have important messages from Jesus Christ. As well as Pope Francis, Fr. Robert Baron, EWTN's Father Cedric, the Franciscan friars, and Mother Angelica. We need to be open enough to listen to all of them. For when Jesus' apostles told Him that "others" are doing miracles in your name, should we stop them? Jesus said, "No, if they are not against us, they are for us."

So, I conclude that Christianity is Christianity; loving the Lord with all your heart, all your soul, and all your strength is all we need. Believing in Jesus Christ's teachings and loving each other as He did, not just talking the talk but walking the walk. That is what should unite all of us.

CPSIA information can be obtained
at www.ICGtesting.com
Printed in the USA
LVHW022124130121
676266LV00007B/178